SHORTSTOP ... OR BUST!

SHORTSTOP ... OR BUST!

The Traveling Tales of Youth Baseball

LINDA PADILLA-DIAZ

iUniverse, Inc.
Bloomington

Shortstop ... or Bust!
The Traveling Tales of Youth Baseball

iUniverse books may be ordered through booksellers or by contacting:

iUniverse
1663 Liberty Drive
Bloomington, IN 47403
www.iuniverse.com
1-800-Authors (1-800-288-4677)

ISBN: 978-1-4759-6501-8 (sc)
ISBN: 978-1-4759-6503-2 (hc)
ISBN: 978-1-4759-6502-5 (e)

Printed in the United States of America

iUniverse rev. date: 1/8/2013

CONTENTS

Foreward

THANKS TO MY FATHER ISMAEL Padilla for his stern command early on in life for my siblings and I to read, read, read which grounded in me a vast love of literature. To my very personal "core four" siblings Mary, Jay, Elsie and Melissa the love, friendship, companionship and continuous desire to celebrate every aspect of our lives is invaluable. A close knit extended Familia of cousins (especially Rachel and Carmen), sisters and brothers-in-law, significant others and close family friends with us and those we sadly lost are forever in my heart.

The next generation of nieces and nephews, DEMENNS (David, Eric, Mark, Evan, Nicky, Nico and Shawn), Sean, Elyse, Ariana, Armand, Liana and Diego, all whom I love like my own, promise to follow your dreams, "keep it going" and always pay it forward. My niece Jillian, the little girl who instantly captured my affection and allowed me to have the daughter I always wanted, holds a special place in my heart. This "fam" is truly privileged to have an impenetrable bond.

My bestie, Ivette Rodriguez Stern, who since we met in the fifth grade has been my confidant, BFF and soul sister, thank you. I don't think I would be who I am today without your friendship. Others in my sisterhood, Ramona, Liz, Denise and Yvonne; I am glad to have you in my life.

My boys provide that precious gift of unqualified love. Children are God's gift to you and what you teach them is your gift to God. I hope through my many loud lectures, speeches, yelling and laughter my boys realize they are MY LIFE. I'm thankful for the greatest career of motherhood.

My hubby/buddy/partner/friend who makes me laugh daily, thank you for your endless support. The hours spent in the dugout solidified an already deep friendship. I'm grateful God gave us another chance when you made it out on that tragic day. May we continue our journey, a day at a time, until the last inning.

Nothing in my life is possible without the matriarch of the family, Carmen Padilla, the epitome of grace, strength and courage under fire. Her sacrifices for her children, grandchildren and family remain endless and her directive to "be the best at what you do, no matter what you do" is the mantra I continue to follow.

"Baseball is just a game….yeah right!"

Introduction

Hello, for your information the team we lost to on Sunday won the tournament; they finished 6–0. That was a good tournament. We had a good time. The boys played well. They didn't win, but the most important thing is that they enjoyed the time in the field, especially playing football at the beach.

YOU WOULD THINK THIS COMMONSENSE, happy thought is at the forefront of every parent's mind. Your kid plays Little League *travel* baseball, and the most important thing is that he or she has fun, right? Now couple the sentiment with a setting in which your child is one of the reasons the team lost a game to knock them out of the competitive tournament. Understandably, as a parent there's an inherent need to spare any blame and justify the loss. As a mom (and more) of the same travel baseball team for the better part of five years, I have seen how the antics, comments, and drama of the parents have reached a peak, resulting in my conclusion that the above noted quote is not a lighthearted, apple-pie prelude to youth travel baseball, but a much needed justification from a parent who believes his child is the second coming of (insert name of any successful major league baseball pitcher/player).

Since I was a child and followed Thurman Munson and the Yankees, I've loved the game of baseball. When pregnant with my first son, Derek, I was placed on strict bed rest and watched Yankee games for the better part of the summer. Could osmosis have been the reason it felt as if Derek grabbed a bat and ball before he could walk? Or more realistically, could Derek's love of the game have been genetically passed on from his dad, who was a Little League maven during his childhood? I fondly recall toddler Derek sitting in his high chair and my husband and I high-fiving each other when he used his *left hand* to pick up his utensil to eat! Yes, baseball has been in our family life from the beginning. It was this love of the game cemented in our household that made the transition in my life to almost daily attendance at youth baseball games an easy one.

Although my childhood was impoverished and we did not have much, my dream was to be on the Supreme Court. When you don't have much, you appreciate what you do have. And a vivid imagination helps. Since I rarely received presents I made presents up. When I opened up a pack of Scott tissue toilet paper, I would thank imaginary friends "Scott and Tiss" for the present! My athletic skills lacked in finesse, and I was more academically than athletically fit. I studied hard, and with the support of a close family network, was the first in my family to go to college. I then obtained a law degree at night, while working during the day as a paralegal in a law firm.

Marrying a baseball fanatic and having two boys totally transformed me, and my priorities shifted. Never in my wildest dreams during my childhood would I have imagined, years later, sitting on a bucket, spitting sunflower seeds and keeping a scorebook for travel baseball teams. As a baseball mom, I've spent many years cheering from a bleacher for my first child and his teammates. I then migrated into the dugout and obtained a different perspective. I expanded by joining the board of the local league and worked with diligent volunteers to ensure that the town kids could play baseball. I took another step and established softball in our league for girls to come out and play. Most of my free time revolves around a ball and a skill where you count balls and strikes. I have little regret and am thankful for the life lessons learned in and around a forty-six-by-sixty-foot diamond filled with dirt and grass.

I am Derek and Luis's baseball mom. My boys are members of youth baseball teams, and, combined, they have played several hundred games, all before the ripe old ages of twelve and fourteen. Derek and Luis play for youth baseball teams managed by their dad, my husband Harry. Harry loves the game of baseball. During his own childhood in the streets of South Bronx, Harry competed successfully in Little League, earning pitching and batting trophies. Harry had a life-changing epiphany on that tragic day in September 2001 and, thankfully, made it out of Tower One, cherishing daily every moment with his boys.

Harry is not a man of many words. Our arguments used to end up with me needing water from thirst while he was cool as a cucumber. I jokingly say his motto (for me) is, "I have nothing to say." His vocabulary when it comes to baseball is endless, and he constantly teaches the game. His sole purpose is to teach kids the game so they can play competitively. Kids like him because he'll speak to them about things they like, such as wrestling and sports. Parents are taken aback; they see him as a little rough around the edges and acerbic, as he'll speak his mind. He is not the pampering type, and to constantly say "it's okay" around him is risky. If you play for Harry, you'll learn the game and collect the hardware (trophies). The old adage says, "Behind every successful man, there's a woman." Well, I'm that woman. I'm secretary, organizer, cupcake baker, e-mail sender, and baseball mom for Harry's teams.

The group of boys that is the subject of this work assembled in 2004 as the "B" town travel team with fourteen kids who had not been selected to the "A" team. They were small. The age group was eight and under (8U), but we had four seven-year-old kids, including my lefty, Derek. In baseball lingo, the seven-year-olds were playing "up." In 2004, they played twenty-two games through three seasons (spring, summer, and fall) and lost more than they won. Talent was evident; polishing was needed. Manager Harry and his squadron of coaches (the joke was there seemed to be a coach per kid; at times we had seven!) dedicated hours to get the kids ready to play competitively. Official coaches were John, Alan, and Nino, and the biggest cheerleader and motivational speaker was Coach Sonny. Later on, Coach Dennis came into the dugout. Game after game, rivalry after rivalry, the team solidified and made noise. They battled, won, and won some more.

I started journaling several years ago, when e-mail updates to relatives about Derek's games ballooned into storytelling. (A note about scores in this book—for simplicity, the team's score will always be reported first.) I compiled stories of a baseball season and was close to sending my collection to print but held back. I would continue to chronicle the games until something monumental happened. Something did happen, but it was not what I expected. Parents tainted my love of the game and hardened my Pollyanna view.

I realize my town is no different than others where moms and dads obsess over baseball, and while many will deny it, the baseball games these boys play between the ages of eight and twelve are the passageway to the ultimate hope of a major league career. After attending many youth baseball games; sitting with, hearing, and observing the coaches and parents; and obtaining a board member's perspective, I have come to believe that youth baseball is not only about the players "having fun" but seems to involve parents' tendencies to live vicariously through their children.

Travel baseball is competitive. Once outside the town recreational arena (where kids are supposed to play regardless of talent), travel baseball is different. You have to try out to make the team, commit to a more extensive practice schedule, and be willing to "travel" to play games. Playing time is not necessarily guaranteed, as the coaches try to put a competitive team on the field. With the competition increasing, it's not uncommon for parents to pay others to teach their children. Also, if a kid isn't allotted the amount of playing time a parent feels is comparable to his or her child's talent or the child isn't made the permanent shortstop or other position of his choice, another team will emerge. Travel baseball teams are established faster than you can say "play ball," and many are considered teams of "daddy ball," where fielding position, batting order, and team revolve around the coach/dad's son. What started as a different venue for competitive play has turned into a moneymaking/expending frenzy, with the goal of having one's child play to win, win, and win, no matter the cost. Loyalty to one team with an attempt to play together consistently has all but vanished, replaced with shopping your stud around for another team to pick him up and play gratis. It is not uncommon for a kid to play on more than one team. If he's good, others will use him as a "guest player," free of charge, while the paying kids sit. I was surprised at the revolution; attending innocent youthful games turned into witnessing the obsession over set positions (parents not kids), hearing Monday morning second-guessing by those who knew more (parents not kids), second-guessing managerial decisions (parents not kids), shopping kids around to other teams, and behind-the-scenes manipulation for an alternative.

It would be unfair to paint a solely negative picture of the beast that is travel baseball. Travel baseball brought me a lot of joy, as the team whose journey this collection chronicles transformed through the years from a "B" team to the team others had to beat. I saw this band of brothers "battle, Tayneck, battle," and memories are priceless. This compilation contains stories from the humble and innocent beginning of the Tayneck travel team and follows the team through competitions and tournaments, successes and disappointments, to its bittersweet end. Apologies are in order, as the vivid enthusiasm evident in the beginning becomes muted. Players came and went, but for the most part a group of kids participated in a ride any sports parent would envy. Harry was at the wheel, and while the ride was a glorious one—with the cheers, bleacher conversations, and rivalries—as expected in any journey, ours was accompanied with bumps; halts; snags; dramatic drops; and, ultimately, a halt.

SUMMER 2005-8U

Prelude with Preston

AFTER A SPRING SEASON OF getting their feet wet, the 8U town travel team entered a local popular tournament, Lincoln Tournament. What would become the norm would be to play several tournaments and juggle many games. They participated in the 8U NJ American Amateur Baseball Congress (AABC) tournament and the Durham Summer tournament, and classic rivalries emerged. Our summer roster consisted of fifteen kids and many coaches, and the squad set out to play many games.

While it seems atypical for seven- and eight-year-olds to play competitively, this group did. In the first game, we were scheduled to play Preston, but were missing four regular players, away on vacation. After the introductory year, the parents hadn't learned the silent rule—you do not go on vacation until summer baseball is over.

Harry (officially manager) and his coaching staff of three coaches (unofficially—seven overzealous dads who wanted to oversee) were ready to compete. After the requisite coin flip, we were designated the visiting team, meaning the other team had the last at bat. I had a bad feeling because I like the last attempt to bat up and score. Tension was high, and nerves were rattled; if you lost, you went into the loser's bracket, and it was really tough to get out of that. Not to mention that the league board of directors had suggested to Harry that it would be nice to win because it had been nine years since the town had won. This was a must win.

The kids played defense like professionals and not the seven- and eight-year-olds they were. Sonny's son, Stefon, pitched three innings, and while parents were a mess, he was calmly blowing bubbles. In the earlier innings, no runs to score had been made on either side. Derek, seven and one of the smallest on the team, played centerfield. Derek and Harry are not tall in stature, but their baseball hearts and guts are the size of any seven-footer. Derek threw a frozen rope from centerfield to second base for the last out in the fifth inning, which did not allow their run to score when the other kid ran from third base. Harry, who normally showed no emotion, was banging the fence with probable pride (which he would never admit). The games are supposed to be six innings, but by the bottom of the sixth, the game was still scoreless—0–0—requiring extra innings. Frazzled nerves, cursing coaches who were being warned to calm down by the umpire, and yelling parents filled the stands, and I felt like I could pee in my pants; my already weakened bladder couldn't handle the pressure. Our kids cried if they struck out or didn't make it on base, but it was the kind of game where both sides were making plays and ensuring that the other side didn't score first. Spectators heard about the 0–0 game and stopped by to watch.

At the top of the seventh, we score, and I have to do everything in my power not to have an accident because my bladder is weak and my heart is racing. As the home team, Preston bats last. Harry brings in a pitcher, Marty, and after two outs, he walks a batter, so the bases are loaded. Harry calls time-out and walks to the mound. The infield joins him, and Harry states, "Get mad; these kids are ready to take *your* game away."

Marty strikes out the next batter; we win and are in the revered winner's bracket! When you win 1–0 in extra innings, as the visiting team missing four regular players, props are in order.

Derek gets the game ball for his play, which prevents a run from scoring. Nice beginning to the tournament!

Edgy with Eastchester

As we moved forward in the winner's bracket, we faced Eastchester. The first game was at a field where spectators sat on opposing bleachers. This game was at another field with one bleacher, which means spectators for both teams sat together! This was not an accommodating setup; every time one of Eastchester's kids was up, the Eastchester spectators were yelling at our kids and vice versa. I almost cursed at a dad who was out of control. Instead, I did the next right thing, and whenever we got a hit or strike out, I yelled, stood up, and waved both arms in the air to block his view. I tried reminding myself not to turn into a psycho mom.

We started with Stefon, the kid blowing bubbles when he was up pitching in the 0–0 game. Harry nicknamed him Steady Stefon. Kids were only allowed to pitch three innings in this tournament, and I'm happy to say that, after three innings, Eastchester had zero, and we'd managed to score three runs in the first three innings. Derek hit a line drive and managed to get to second base. This made up for the bobble to him in the first inning while at second base, which had allowed a kid to get on base but thankfully not to score.

In the fourth inning, we bring in Sosa who was away all week and possibly rusty. A couple of sloppy plays, and Eastchester scores two runs, bringing the score to 3–2. Since I have no more nails to bite, I start with sunflower seeds, and the sodium is running through my body. I feel my fingers swell. However, we get through that inning and are ahead.

At the top of the fifth, they bring in "Mikey." His dad is behind me, and I hear "C'mon, Mikey, give them what you got; they can't hit you!" We hit and score four runs, bringing the score to 7–2.

In the bottom fifth, our hero from the Preston game is pitching. Marty walks a couple, and they score. Another kid scores, although Derek throws a laser from second base to the catcher, who catches it, but stands with it and forgets to tag the runner. 7–4.

During the top sixth, we don't score. One of our moms is on the phone asking for updates and makes me stay on the phone to do a play-by-play. Marty comes back to pitch the bottom of the sixth, but it's evident he doesn't have it. In comes Wamcash, whom I affectionately call our Mariano. In my mind, all that is needed is the introductory music! Harry gives him the ball, says something magical, and off he goes. Strikes out two right away. Mikey's dad is in front of me in the first row of the bleachers (probably moved because I stood too many times), and Wamcash does it—he strikes out the third batter, and we win 7–4. The mothers start yelling and clapping; Derek sees us and smiles from the field and suggests we stand up! What a game. Not as pretty as the first one but effective.

Next up: last year's champion—Oxford!

Outstanding versus Oxford

LET ME PUT IN PERSPECTIVE how big this game was. I forfeited my own women's softball game, sat for two hours with Luis (with combined smells of chlorine and sunscreen from camp) because he took a nap and was cranky when I woke him up, and had PMS but still sat with the spectators from the other team, although I walked away when I didn't know if I was going to yell, cry, or do both.

My family had arrived early, so I'd seen the Oxford team practice for about forty minutes, and I was nervous (I'm not sure if it was the PMS hormones or the smell of chlorine penetrating my brain cells). They looked like the champions they were (last year's). I told one of the moms they looked good, and she went pale.

With the coin toss, we are the visiting team and bat up first. In the first inning, Jack earns a walk from the pitcher, who looks like the mean kid in *Leave it to Beaver* and has the weirdest pitching stance. Derek smacks a line drive, but the second baseman snatches it (I said they were good), and Jack stays on first. Marty strikes out, and Stefon earns a walk. Two outs, runners on first and second, and up comes Wamcash. He smacks the ball to the outfield, and the kids run. Harry (whom I nicknamed "the mad waver" since he's always waving the players to home plate) waves Wamcash home. Beaver stands on the white line in front of the catcher, and Wamcash goes around him and slides home. The pitcher is called with interference, and we're up 3–0 in the bottom of the first inning.

Stefon is pitching at the bottom of the first but is giving up walks. Harry later tells me this kid gave him six straight shutout innings of baseball the first two days, and even Roger Clemens has bad outings. They score two in the first inning, and we are leading 3–2.

During the second inning, neither team scores. Beaver and Stefon are still pitchers of record. I notice Derek doing something new as he walks out of the dugout to bat (making the sign of the cross), and I wonder whether he's watching too many ESPN highlights. At the bottom of the third, Oxford bats, and Stefon allows a run; the game is tied. I take Luis for his first trip to the canteen (it's about 8:30, and he tells me, "I think I'm awake now") and see Derek warming up with Harry in the dugout, and my heart falls. I can't believe he's bringing in the Little Unit (Derek), and I worry the game may get out of hand because, during the warm-up pitches, he's throwing a lot of balls. I call out, "Are you serious?" But Harry doesn't hear me (or more likely ignores me). Luis gets his hot dog. My heart is aflutter. I head back to my bleacher seat and don't tell the spectators what I think is going to happen. This is a tied ball game; why not bring in Mariano? The announcement is made about the pitching change, and it's Jack (whew!). Jack strikes out the batter; the game remains tied.

In the top fourth, we don't score, and the dreaded feeling of the possibility of another tie looms, which my nerves and bladder can't handle (although this time I brought extra panty liners). Jack is still pitching, and an error by the first baseman allows the kid to get to second base. The second batter hits another double and brings in the runner. They're leading 3–4. Their parents (and they had a lot more people there) were wild. Harry calls time and brings in Wamcash. Although they have a runner on second, he strikes out three in a row to End the inning 3–4.

It's the top fifth, and before the kids come out to bat, Harry stops them and yells, "*This is your inning!*"

They respond with many hits. Oxford's new pitcher is throwing hard but a little wild. We score five runs in the top of the fifth with a smashing single by Stan, which should have been a double, but he's not known for his speed. His dad, the quietest guy on the bleachers, goes ballistic yelling. The inning's over, and we lead 8–4.

I and another mom start calling out to any baseball god for help. Another vacation mom is calling with her son for updates, and the mom and absent player want to stay on the phone for a play-by-play (I wonder about my cell phone bill!). During the top sixth, we don't score. The score remains 8–4.

Wamcash allows a runner on first but then strikes out three. The inning's over; we win. We're not as obnoxious with our chants (they did outnumber us), but we share in a lot of high-fiving and hugging. The out-of-town player hears the announcement of a Sunday game, and I'm assured he'll be back in time!

Routed by Riverhead

I'M A FIRM BELIEVER IN superstition, and on the day we were scheduled to play Riverhead, things seemed like they were going wrong. Harry never spoke to his coaches on game day. Out in the backyard, no sooner did I remind Harry of this than Coach John called. How bad could it be? Let them talk.

Twenty minutes later, Coach Alan called to say he'd landed safely and would be at the game with his son. I thought about saying, "Okay, I'll tell him," but instead said, "Let me put Harry on the phone."

To top it off, I usually bought a big pack of Juicy Fruit gum to give to each kid, telling them it was "hitting gum" (that always brought a smile). Pathmark didn't have Juicy Fruit, and I forgot to get it elsewhere! We had also been the visiting team the past three (successful) games but now were home. I had a yucky feeling before the game started.

Plain and simple, the Riverhead team was good. This team played in last year's championship game and lost. I believe they wanted it. Their pitcher was a youthful combination of Clemens/Johnson/Schilling and pitched fast—not to mention our kids weren't chewing hitting gum, which put a damper on everything!

The bases are loaded in the second inning; their batter hits to our shortstop, who catches it but throws it pretty high to the second baseman. And although the latter has it, it falls out of his glove. One runner scores. Their next batter hits a shot that scores three more, moving the score to 0–4. We even have hornets, bees, or some other bug buzzing in right field that sent Stan running out because he thought he would get stung. He sat out of the dugout until it was time for him to hit.

Not even our own Mariano can stop the scoring machine that is Riverhead. The final score, 0–8. Yep, we were shut out. One of our siblings previously coined the phrase "give them the medicine," and that night was our turn to get some.

However, it's not over. Riverhead goes to the championship, and we have to play Oxford, whom we'd previously beaten 8–4. The winner of that game plays Riverhead. Out of fourteen teams, three are left. If nothing else, our kids have displayed dedication, persistence, and outright guts in this quest. Harry says all he's going to do is tell them do their best and have fun. Just in case, I plan to have the Juicy Fruit with my sunflower seeds.

End of Superstition?

I TRIED MY DARNDEST TO keep the superstition going—had the Juicy Fruit, kept the coaches from speaking—but it was tough. *Wives* were calling each other to determine which shirts the coaches should wear. When Coach John called and I told him he couldn't speak to Harry, he laughed but told me they needed to discuss the lineup. "Okay," I said hesitantly (while cursing under my breath) and decided to hell with the same outfit I had been continuously wearing (cleaned of course).

The team wore white T-shirts under their vests for home games and red T-shirts under the vests for away games. Some heard Harry say white for this game, but others arrived in red shirts; some of our coaches wore black shirts, and some wore white shirts. We were uncoordinated. I questioned Harry about it, and he replied, "I don't give a damn what they're wearing, so long as they play baseball." He's not a man of many words.

We arrived at the bleachers, and the Oxford families (the nicest group of fans encountered) were in the front row with pom-poms! They outnumbered us, but the moms took the same seats, pulled out sunflower seeds, and awaited the game. I realized I still had the gum(!), panicked, and ran to the dugout with Luis. I tried to hide that I was giving out the "hitting gum" before the coordinator threw me and Luis out. I told Edgar to give out the gum and make sure he called it "hitting gum." As we were running out, Luis said, "Edgar's probably gonna eat all the gum, right?" And my heart sank.

Coin toss done, we are the visiting team. Jack strikes out, and Derek walks. Marty gets a hit, and third-base coach Harry is yelling at Derek to stay at second. Derek doesn't listen, runs, and slides into third but is tagged out. Two outs, Marty on first, and Stefon hits an infield grounder ending the inning. We take the field, and I don't see Derek at second because he's in the dugout crying and blaming Harry for getting tagged out! Jason, on return from his vacation, is set to pitch; he walks a batter and gives up a couple of hits. The score is 0–2. Pom-poms are soaring, making me want to throw a match in the air. Not again.

At the top of the second, Wamcash walks. Edgar (the gum recipient) is up and gets a nice hit to the outfield (it worked!). Wamcash makes it to third. Jacob strikes out, and Stan whacks the ball to the outfield, bringing Wamcash in and the score to 2–2.

With our pitching at the bottom second and bottom third and fantastic defense, we hold them at 2. We get another run, courtesy of Stefon, who brings a batter in, and the score is 3–2. We're not getting any more runs because the defensive plays are phenomenal. At the top of the fourth, we earn another run, bringing the score to 4–2.

The Oxford moms start singing, "Here we go, Oxford, here we go," and we're yelling on top of them, *"Defense! Defense!"* Marty comes in to pitch and does not allow a run. We're up to bat, it's the bottom fourth, and we start singing, "Here we go, Tayneck, here we go!"

The dad in the stand behind us yells, "Don't let them take your song!" They start waving pom-poms.

No runs, and we go to the top of the fifth, leaving bases loaded without scoring a run. In the bottom five, Marty does the job, assisted by a fantastic play at second from Derek (who's no longer crying but has assumed his position at second) to shortstop Wamcash for an out at second. Wamcash attempts to convert to a double play at first, but the runner is called safe.

At the top of the sixth, I'm nervous and seeds are spit all over the place. After a parent observes my spit fest, I promise to attend Sunflower Seeds Anonymous. Soon, it's the bottom sixth, and up to bat is the top of the lineup. Mariano Wamcash comes in (in my mind, I hear the entrance music) and strikes out the first batter. Wamcash's mom, sitting next to me, starts doing her happy dance, and an Oxford dad yells, "Hey, you can't do the happy dance!" I ask her to sit before we get jinxed. The second batter walks; I told her not to dance! The third batter hits a shot to left field, but our defender makes the catch. With two outs and a runner on first, batter number four strikes out. We win, 4–2. We're hugging and high-fiving, and the classy parents at Oxford tell us, "Good job. Go all the way and win."

While Oxford was receiving their trophies, we were told we would play Riverhead. Out of fourteen teams, two were left. I felt reasonable and said, "If they don't win, so what"—until I overheard a Riverhead player (whose dad was watching the game and taking notes) say, "So we beat Tayneck, and this is the end for them." All thoughts of reasonableness were gone. I wanted to beat this team badly!

Unfortunately, our boys didn't win, losing 3–5 and taking second place. Considering the prior year when we were eliminated quickly, this was a nice end.

We had to prepare for other games in the tournament play-offs. Next, we would face our township rivals in the semifinals.

Dead End at Durham

DURING THE SUMMER SEASON IN one of the many leagues, we were undefeated. A memorable game against Allendale taught me something about Harry. Derek was the starting pitcher and, in the first inning, allowed ten runs. I was seething with rage and embarrassment because that was *my kid* on the mound who I felt was being embarrassed. Derek was fine. Harry told me that, after that atrocious outing, when we had to take the field again the following inning, Derek said, "Coach, am I still pitching?" (No!) We won the game, and later on that evening, I asked Harry why he wouldn't take Derek out if he was struggling. He replied, "If I take a pitcher out when it gets hard, what is that going to teach him?" I realized he truly had an interest in teaching the kids to compete but also in establishing some baseball bravado.

We made it to the championship game, beating a township rival, and hung around to watch the remaining teams to determine who our next opponent would be. We left when Preston was winning 8–1. Given that we played Preston in game one of the Lincoln Tournament and successfully moved into the winner's bracket while they went to the loser's bracket, I'm sure they practiced with a picture of our team in front of their dugout.

The championship game was scheduled for 6:00 p.m., and given my gnawing superstition, I wore the same shorts and sandals I'd been wearing most of the season. Coach John (away out of town) e-mailed parents asking them to wear red, prompting a mom to write a frantic e-mail pleading for no one to wear red because, last time we did, we got whooped by Riverhead. Another dad sent his e-mail stating that, since we'd won on Sunday, we should do the same things, and I wondered if this superstition was getting out of hand. Therefore, I didn't wear red, and I didn't bring the guacamole and chips as ordered.

Harry starts with Stefon, who walks two and bobbles a blooper to the pitcher's mound; the bases are loaded. This is a championship game, so Harry takes no chances and takes Stefon out (not allowing for bad days today). In comes Sosa, who throws strikes the opponents are hitting, but our defense isn't catching the balls. By the top of the second inning, Preston is ahead 0–6. I'm popping and spitting sunflower seeds, and some moms suggest the game is over, prompting me to yell, "Would you stop? The game is six innings, eighteen outs. Don't give up on the kids."

Stunned and shocked, the parents around me mumble replies, but they cheer. My yells consisted of reminding our kids they have bats too, which was scaring the Preston pitcher, who kept looking my way!

We hit, and by bottom of the second, we score; now it's 1–6.

At the top of the third, we change pitchers, but there are bunts and bloops we don't handle, and the score is 1–8. At the bottom of the third, we have bases loaded, and Stefon gets a hit that allows the third-base runner to score (2–8). But Jack (who could earn Oscars for his performances) runs into the shortstop and lands on the ground between second and third, wailing! The moms wonder, "Is he okay?" Angrily, I say, "I'm sure he's fine." But I see Coach Alan carry him off the field (reminiscent of Richard Gere carrying Debra Winger off in *An Officer and a Gentleman*), and I wonder whether I was harsh. Before he's carried off and while he's on the ground writhing in pain, the first baseman grabs the ball and gingerly tags Jack out, as the ball is still considered in play. Heartless, yes, but necessary, as time-out was not called.

At the top of the fourth, we bring in Wamcash. Strangely, the other team is hitting the ball, and Wamcash does not seem as invincible as he's been the past couple of games. By the bottom of the fifth, the score is 4–11.

The bottom of the sixth—our last inning, our only chance—arrives, and Jack (he's fine of course) walks. Derek is up and smacks it to the outfield. He is dancing on first. Since Derek always motions for us to cheer, when he comes up, I tell the parents around me to yell for him. After a great hit, he is dancing nervously but not because he's excited from our cheers. Rather, he seems to have inherited Mom's weak bladder! Marty hits, sending Derek to second, and Wamcash hits, so Derek's on third. The bases are loaded; could it be a miracle is in the works?

With two outs, Stefon smacks the ball, and Harry (positioned at third base) sends Derek, tells him to *stop* and then sends him again—into the hands of the opposing catcher, gleefully waiting at home to tag him out. Preston wins 5–11. Second place again?! Coach John, who is away receiving phone play-by-plays, says he's going to go drink with Jack (Daniels).

Harry proclaimed, "You never want to have the last out at third base," and beat himself up for sending, stopping, and sending Derek to home. Derek felt bad, but Harry lovingly told him he would gladly take ten Dereks on his team because he shows up to play all the time. Derek's reaction of bashful pride was touching.

I was sad for Harry because he'd had two opportunities to bring home a championship for our "little warriors" (as they were soon penned), neither of which materialized. I knew Harry was upset, but I was surprised at how down, gloomy, and cheerless I felt. For the third time this baseball season (twice in four days), we had come in second place.

In the overall scheme of things, youth baseball and its losses are not significant, but I felt like we were the perpetual bridesmaid who would never be a bride. Harry, dedicated manager, third-base coach, mad waver, and Zen leader, said, teary eyed, "You can't make it to the Big Dance [twice] and not win."

Notwithstanding the fact that our kids had been in two championship games in four days and had played against sixteen teams for the past month—an outstanding feat in and of itself—it was like we'd hit the ceiling, and it wasn't glass but cement. During the games, I'd been talking to God and saying, "Whatever happens is meant to happen." But I was staggered by the fact we couldn't win a tournament.

This was the part where you would say there were things more important in life, yada, yada, but it sucked coming in second again. I felt like it was 2004 when the Yankees lost to the Red Sox after leading the American League Championship series 3–0 (we were undefeated in the tournament) and hoped it didn't last long (it was a long winter). I reluctantly went to the pitcher I'd scared and told him he pitched a fantastic game. He didn't seem so afraid.

No tears were shed among the team—the boys were just playing in the playground—although the siblings, including Luis, were sad. Did they want to win? Were they tired from camp? Was it too much baseball? No one knew. We went to Dairy Queen, and while the kids had ice cream, the parents rehashed plays of the game. "If he'd thrown a strike here …" "If he'd caught the ball …" "If only he hadn't sent him from third …"

Harry was annoyed. What else could he do? We had no problem getting to the championship, we had pitching and hitting, but it was winning that thwarted us. Without another explanation, I started blaming our zip code (07666) and thought about petitioning the mayor to change the last three digits because I thought we were cursed.

I would do my damnedest to make sure Derek had fun, kid fun for the rest of August because fall baseball would start in September. I was anxious; in the fall, the teams "moved up" in age classifications (so we would be 9U, while Derek was still really eight). And while I believed Derek could handle it, I wasn't sure what the others thought, especially after that last out. Harry reminded me, "Derek's a player" and could hold his own.

I'm an optimist, and I remembered that I'd been a bridesmaid seven times before I'd married Harry. I knew he was hurting. We usually spent hours talking about the games (baseball is the foundation of our marriage). But after this loss, he slept without talking. I would love for him to be rewarded with a first-place trophy; he had taken this group of kids with a losing record and quickly turned them around to be the team everyone wanted to beat. The kids loved him, the coaches admired him (I think), and some of the moms cooked fancy desserts for him. I knew God had an ultimate plan, and that I could go back to whatever happens happens, but I couldn't shake that gnawing feeling of having come in second place. It would pass—all bad feelings do—but shit, second place …

FALL 2005-8U

Confused with Clarkson

AFTER CONSECUTIVE CHAMPIONSHIP LOSSES, WE took a break before fall baseball. Some of the team members played football and soccer, but many remained dedicated to playing baseball. So Harry signed them up for a fall tournament starting September 2005. Harry would bat all thirteen players in the lineup. Teams played approximately eight games for seeding and then started play-offs.

We played Clarkson, and my mom and I were in the scoring box talking baseball (peculiar indeed). The field scoreboard was missing a lightbulb on a panel, so one lightbulb was lit, even if there were two outs. I alerted the opposing team. The umpire was intent on teaching the kids the "ethics" of baseball, such as the sin of arguing balls and strikes, prompting him to stop the game every couple of minutes; we'd only played four innings, although the team had been on the field for two hours and had played sloppily. Derek committed about five errors, so I asked what happened. "I don't want to talk about it," he said. Eight-year-olds have bad days too.

This game was a rescheduled game that Harry was not expected to attend, and he'd told Coach John to run the game. John discussed the rules with the opposing coach. When Harry unexpectedly got to the third-base coaching area, he was clueless as to the rules the two coaches had discussed. This would come into play later.

Jason starts and strikes out two. Batter number three hits a bullet to second base, but Derek fails to keep his glove down and it goes through his legs (Bill Buckner?). Thereafter, Jason walked more, and the score was 0–3. Harry talks to Jason, but more walks ensue, as do more errors. Soon, the lead is 0–6 in the top of the first. I asked Harry why he would keep Jason in, and Harry said something like, "Kids gotta learn …"

A tall, lanky kid is pitching for Clarkson but not before the manager argues the pitcher's mound is "not right," because his foot kept slipping—something about being tall like Randy Johnson and needing more dirt on the mound (what?). We stop the game four times to get dirt on the mound, and in between, Jack and Derek walk on base. Wamcash strikes out. Three consecutive walks are next, and by the end of the fifty-minute first inning, the score is 3–6.

At the top of the second, it appears Jason didn't have to learn anymore. Harry brings in Sosa, who throws strikes, but the kids hit. Another error, and they score two; it's 3–8.

The bottom of the second and they switch pitchers, as the mound still isn't "good enough." We steal, we hit, we walk, and by the end of the inning, we've tied the game 8–8. Parents are wild, and the opposing coaches question why we are cheering! What, are we watching golf?

In the top of the third, they get some hits, and we make a couple of errors. That, in combination with the hovering full moon, allows Clarkson to score seven runs before the inning's over; 15–8.

The bottom of the third—*our* boys score seven runs to tie the game. One of the Clarkson coaches questions the umpire, prompting him to yell and throw the coach out. I'm still keeping the scoreboard but not fast enough, as a player is yelling at me about the score. I yell, "I know what I'm doing!"

Stan hits a blast to the outfield that could have been a home run if he were lighter on his feet. The obnoxious dad yells to the umpire about two outs (because he only sees one lightbulb). And I yell, "I know; it's been announced!"

The inning's over. The umpire decides to allow one more inning because it's after nine.

For the top of the fourth, we bring in Mariano, and he makes up for the two strikeouts he had early in the game. He fans two batters immediately, and the third batter hits a bullet to third, where trusty Sosa throws himself on top of it and gets it to first for their last out.

We bat up last. Marty gets a bloop single and steals two bases, so he's at third. We need one run to win the game. Stefon strikes out, and Edgar earns a walk. The rules the coaches discussed earlier allow a walk to run to second base as long as the pitcher doesn't have the ball. Edgar starts running to second and Harry, who missed the rules, yells *"What are you doing?"* The plan was to get the catcher to throw the ball to second to get him out, so that Marty could run home and score the game winning run. So while Harry's yelling at Edgar, Marty is stuck at third with two outs. The coaches are yelling at each other back and forth. The third batter, Mac, strikes out; the game is over, and we're tied.

We had the game, but communication was missing. Although the umpire tried to teach the kids how to act, I'm not sure it made an impact, as the parents left still cussing the umpire. I got a brief glimpse at how serious parents take these games. It was scary.

Play-offs—The Angry First-Base Coach

THE PLAY-OFFS WERE SINGLE ELIMINATION; if you lost, you went home. We ended the fall season with a record of 5–2–1 (five wins, two losses, and one tie) and captured third place. For the first round of the play-offs, we played the fifth-place team—our rival, Preston. I compared Preston vs. Tayneck to Yankees vs. Red Sox—not much love lost, sporadic controversy, and an occasional coach being thrown out of the game. We beat them in Lincoln, they beat us during the summer championship game, and we were meeting again for the rubber game.

Our home game was scheduled for Saturday, but as the area was inundated with rain, the possibility of playing on our field on the first dry afternoon was slim. After much rearranging, the game was rescheduled for 7:00 p.m., and we had to play elsewhere.

We got to the field at 6:15 p.m. Some parents felt 7:00 p.m. was too late for their youngsters, who should be in bed by 9:00 p.m. It was fall, so spectators were sitting in cold metal bleachers for several hours at night. Because of another game going on, we didn't start at 7:00 p.m. but closer to 8:00. Parents were not happy.

As the higher-seeded home team, we take the field first, and Preston bats up first. Our ole reliable Sosa is on the mound, throwing smoke. However, where there are errors, you get runs. Mac, who's playing shortstop, gets a "bad hop" (according to his dad, who proclaims to the parents in the bleachers that it wasn't his fault) and loses the ball. Harry, who has sharp hearing, hears the proclamation, and giving his expected honest opinion, abruptly states, "It's not a bad hop; it's an error."

By the top of the second inning, Preston is leading 0–3. The thought of Preston beating us in two play-off games in the same decade (never mind the same year) is too much for my cold ass (literally) to take. Unlike our other games when our parents led the cheers, something different is happening. The Preston parents are cheering, and I say to a mom, "Oh, they better not think they can cheer louder than us."

In the bottom of the second our kids hit, and balls are slammed all over the field. We tie the game, and it's 3–3. The umpire stops the game to indicate that the players can't cheer, prompting the crazy parents to start chanting "First Amendment, First Amendment!" If our kids can't cheer, we will.

We switch pitchers and bring in Mac. Preston's big kid hitter (who has safely hit in every game I've seen) slams the ball to the left field. Preston starts cheering; Stan, in left field, is bobbling, trying to get the ball, and gets it to the cutoff Sosa, who throws a frozen rope to third baseman (Wamcash); Wamcash tags the kid out. We go nuts, and they stop cheering. That play keeps the game tied. Two more outs follow, and we're up to bat in the bottom of the third.

Our first-base coach, Alan, is away for the unfortunate death of a relative, which brings Coach John (who usually keeps the scorebook) to coach first base. Similar to Harry, Coach John is a get-in-your-face guy who speaks his mind. We score two more runs, and up to bat is Jacob, who hits and gets to first base. Stan hits a blooper, and John is yelling, I mean *yelling*, at Jacob to run. For whatever reason (fear?), Jacob doesn't run and John *pushes him* off of first base. Parents are yelling—"What the hell did he do that for?!" And suddenly, the umpire goes to the pitcher's mound and stops everything. He calls Jacob out, since Coach John touched him, which is not allowed.

Harry runs over to John and says, "It's okay if the kids lose the game, but let's not have the coaches do anything to lose the game."

To that, John responds, "Don't talk to me."

The pitcher holds them.

At the bottom of the fourth, John walks to the bleachers. Seeing the cold moms huddled in blankets, he asks, "You guys cold?"

"We're just sitting here," I reply. "You're actively keeping warm by pushing kids off first base."

He walks away mumbling.

We score more runs that inning, and the score is 12–3.

At the top of the fifth, we bring in Wamcash, who holds them but not without Coach John yelling, *"Just throw strikes!"*

We come to bat and score three more, bringing the score to 15–3. The inning is peppered with another ranting session from John. He yells at Eddie, who hits a shot to right field but runs slowly. When Eddie barely gets to first base, John yells that he has to run and not stop. Eddie gives him a blank stare.

I go to John's wife and say, "Unlike Alan, John's an angry first-base coach."

She laughs and agrees.

In the top of the sixth, Preston bats, but with Wamcash's great pitching, they don't score.

The game over, Tayneck wins, and we get a chance at the semifinals.

Play-offs—Semifinals and Havoc with Hartford

IT WAS A COLD NIGHT (in the 40s), but since we'd had so much rain we had to get the game in and were forced to play. Derek wore pajamas underneath his uniform and a black turtleneck underneath his vest. Coach John previously suggested the fans wear red, but with our sweatshirts, jackets, gloves, and hats, the only thing red were our cheeks (both sides)!

Hartford previously beat us 7–10, scoring the three runs in the last inning. One of their players was a big kid I affectionately call Galoopa! Could he be nine? The last time we'd played, I'd been in the scorer's booth with a couple of moms and, according to their coach, (who also happened to be Galoopa's dad) we were making him nervous with our cheers. The umpire directed us not to cheer. I (as did others) secretly cheered my loudest; my jugular actually hurt.

At the top of the first—we're the away team (because Hartford had a better record)—we start with numbers 1 and 2. They both walk, taking first and second bases. Harry likes to steal bases. Stan's dad yells, "Let the running begin!" Wamcash strikes out, but the others steal. Sosa hits a double, scoring Jack. Derek's now at third, and the score is 1–0.

The bottom of the first—Sosa pitches and has a quick inning.

At the top of the second, Edgar strikes out, Mac walks, and Stan doubles. The Hartford coach is yelling at his players, "Talk it up!" for their pitcher. They yell, "Come on; they can't hit you!"

Jacob hits a line drive to the third baseman, who makes a great catch.

It's the bottom of the second, and Sosa's still pitching. The batter pops up to second, where Marty appears to catch it. But Jacob bumps into him, and the ball falls out of his glove. With a runner on first, Sosa walks the next two batters, and the bases are loaded. Their fourth batter hits a ball to the pitcher, but Sosa makes a wild throw to the catcher, and they score two, giving Hartford a 1–2 lead.

At the top of the third, Eddie hits directly to the pitcher, and he's out. D-Rod, who was out for three weeks with stitches, walks, as does Jack. Derek, on a 3–2 count, earns a walk. Not knowing if it's a walk or a foul, he runs to first base but has the bat in hand. The umpire calls him out! Apparently, running to first base with the bat is an automatic out. Wamcash strikes out. Moms start saying, "Oh man, that was big for us, that call." I'm thinking they mean Derek's mistake was big, and I'm embarrassed.

Bottom third—the score is 1–2. Mac, the quietest kid, is pitching and smiles shyly every time I yell, "Come on, Mighty Mac!" Kids are blowing into their hands because it's cold, and the big Galoopa coach is on third base, giving hand signals to all his players, who gaze at him. I wish Harry would do something fancy with the hand signals. Mac strikes out the first batter. The player bunts and gets to first. After a wild pitch, he steals second, but Mac gets the other guy out. Big Galoopa gets intentionally walked, and the coach is angry. Coach Nino pleasantly supports Harry, stating, "Never mind. That's baseball strategy." After a ground out, the inning comes to an end.

At the top of the fourth, Sosa hits a line drive to the outfield. He gets to third base, and Harry almost hugs him. As the defense unsuccessfully tries to get Jason out at second, Sosa scores; the game is tied at 2–2. Stefon hits a double, scoring Jason. The quiet dad yells, "Everybody gets a hit!" I suggest maybe stomping feet on the metal bleachers might be a bit much. Edgar bunts and gets to second, and Stan hits and scores Stefon. Edgar scores, and now we're up 5–2.

Mac's back on the pitcher's mound for the bottom of the fourth. Jason's mom puts on a DVD in her car so the siblings can warm up (which has the bonus of preventing Luis from eating every ten minutes). Hartford hits a line drive to the shortstop, and Sosa gets the runner out at first. At the inning's end, the score is 5–3.

At the top of the fifth, Hartford has a new pitcher. We get to first on a line drive. D-Rod's up, and Coach Harry gives him "invisible" signs (thank you!). He places a beautiful bunt (yes, I think bunts are beautiful). He makes it to third base on the bunt, and we score. Jack walks, and Derek's up.

I'm praying to the baseball gods (*please let him make up for that mistake*). But he strikes out. Wamcash is up, and a wild pitch is thrown, but I'm watching Harry send D-Rod home. D-Rod hesitates back and forth between third and home, and Hartford gets him out. Why, oh why is he always sending kids home? With two outs, Sosa steps to the plate; he doubles, scoring two, and we're at 8–3.

Wamcash pitches the bottom of the fifth. Derek wants to contribute and starts hounding Harry to let him pitch. "Warm me up," he says. "I can get the job done." Wamcash is struggling; it seems the pressure is getting to him. I can't tell how kids got on base because I walk back to the canteen with Luis for another snack.

At the top of the sixth, Galoopa is pitching. Jason walks, Marty gets a wild pitch, and Jason steals second. Big dad/coach goes to the pitcher, and he points at us. I guess we're bothering him again. Mac's dad reminds us we taunted him at the last game, making me yell, "We didn't do shit to him! If he can't take it, he shouldn't play baseball." I silently remind myself not to be a psycho mom. Marty strikes out, but Stefon hits and we have runners on first and third. Edgar gets a pitch to the head, but he's okay and at first. The bases are loaded. Mac hits and scores Jason. Stefon steals home, and we're up 10–3.

In the bottom of the sixth, Wamcash is still in, but Derek wants to pitch, and he's following Harry around with his glove. I walk to Derek and say, "*Stop it!* Leave Dad alone," because I think Harry threatened to throw him out of the dugout. Wamcash is throwing haphazardly, and Harry, crouched outside of the dugout, waves his hands furiously. "Just throw strikes!" The ball gets to Wamcash but it's dropped. The next kid hits a line drive triple, and Hartford scores. Harry paces quickly with a glove, Derek running behind him for a warm-up.

When a line drive comes to our shortstop, he throws it wildly to first base, and Hartford scores; now it's 10–5. The next batter's out, so we need two outs to make it to the championship. But Wamcash walks two batters! I'm too nervous to sit with the moms, so I walk to the dugout and see Alan hiding because he says he can't watch. Harry is pleading with Wamcash, "Just throw strikes."

Coach John arrives at the field directly from the airport, and since I'm near the dugout, I update him on what's going on. One of the moms says things will be okay as all the coaches are here (superstition), and I secretly hope Coach John's presence gets Wamcash to throw strikes because Harry's pleading is not working.

Harry walks to the mound, and the infield joins him for a pep talk. He tells them to relax. The third-base coach is giving so many hand signals he looks like a mime. Derek wants to pitch.

What happens next? Luis, along with two other team siblings, comes running out of the car telling me he needs the bathroom, so I take the kids to the bathroom. By the time we're done, I see the kids lining up to shake hands. Could it be!? We won, and in dramatic fashion.

I learned that Big Galoopa batted with runners on second and third, two outs, and the score at 10–5. Wamcash threw a wild pitch, and the coach sent the kid to steal home. All Harry heard was, "Get him, Jay!" And he grabbed the ball, ran to the plate, and waited to tag the runner out. Game over.

The teams lined up, and Hartford's coach didn't shake Harry's hand. Harry told me he'd overheard this coach telling his parents, "I beat him [Harry] at his game," when he beat us at our field.

I was proud of the way the game was managed, played, and won. Derek had a bad day, as did Wamcash, but I reminded him that *the team* won. This team had made it to five championship games in less than five months. We'd come in second four times. Could the fifth be the charm?

A Scary Halloween Eve!

THE CHAMPIONSHIP GAME ORIGINALLY SCHEDULED for Saturday was switched to Sunday when Sosa's mom heard a favorable weather forecast. She was right, as the weather was magnificent. Luis yelled, "Stop saying that!" after I greeted everyone (those on the other team included) with "Great day for baseball." He's not one for small talk. My sisters and mother were expected, and others had the same idea; grandmas, cousins, and friends were there to cheer the boys on. Some came with banners we tried posting on the field. This was it—championship baseball (albeit youth) in October.

I was nervous. I had pen and paper in hand but must say it was pretty useless because, in looking at my notes to later compile a story, I saw chicken scratch that would make any doctor proud. I got to the field early, took Luis to the playground, and gave him two dollars to start so he could get something to eat. We were the visiting team. I heard Harry speaking to the boys in left field. "There are eighteen outs in the game, and we're going to play hard from out number one to out number eighteen," he told them.

The coaches did their routine cheer. "One-two-three, *Tayneck!*"

Jack walks and is able to steal second and third. However, Derek, Sosa, and Wamcash strike out.

In the bottom of the first, Sosa pitches. On his first pitch to batter number one, the batter hits a sinking line drive to left field. Derek has been relegated to left field despite his preference for infield. But he is a champ and a team player and guards left field voraciously. His catch is phenomenal. He keeps his eye on the ball, runs to catch it, and slides on the ground to meet up with it, hitting the ground and holding it. We go ballistic, and the first thing I think of is "redemption."

Yankee fans may remember when Chuck Knoblauch made an error during a play-off game at second base. He came back the next game to hit a home run to tie an otherwise dismal game and was asked whether he felt redemption. He denied it. I'm sure Derek isn't thinking like that, but I am, and it feels good. Derek has not been hitting well, so to have him do something to help the team is gratifying. What a smile on his face when he hears the fans yelling, "Way to go, Double D!" The second batter hits a pop blooper to first base, but the ball drops in front of Jacob; the batter's safe on first. The second batter strikes out, and a third out is made; the score is 0–0.

At the top of the second, Jason strikes out; Marty walks. Stefon strikes out; Marty steals a base. And while Edgar walks, Marty steals home; it's 1–0. Mac strikes out.

It's the bottom of the second. Sosa is still pitching, and the batter hits to our shortstop. He mistakenly overthrows to first, and the runner ends up on third base. The next batter hits to third, and he's out at first but not before they tie the score, 1–1.

Harry goes up to give a pep talk. Sosa is complaining he's hot (he's wearing a black turtleneck). Harry tells him, "Well, you can't take your shirt off now," and walks off.

Harry gets Derek out of left to warm him up and puts the pitcher in left field. They score again and by the inning's end are leading 1–4.

At the top of the third, Stan hits to the third baseman, who makes the easy throw to first base—one out. Jacob hits to the pitcher, who makes another easy throw to first base—two outs. Eddie hits to the third baseman, and again, the throw to first is an easy one, and we're at three outs. These kids are converting basic plays to get the outs, and we're making errors. I see Harry has not let go of the baseball bat he has been carrying the whole game and begin to worry about what he's thinking.

In the bottom of the third, Mac is pitching. But I can't tell what happens because my family arrived. I was busy getting chairs set up and making sure everybody knew where the bathroom was (Luis told them where the canteen was). According to Harry, they scored another run on a walk, so in the bottom of the third, the score is 1–5.

At the top of the fourth, we're in the hole. Remember, they'll bat last, and we need to come up with four runs to tie the game. Their pitching is unbelievable, so the prospect is scary. D-Rod walks. We're at the top of the lineup. Jack bunts, but D-Rod runs slow, so they get him out at second. Derek walks and moves Jack to second. Wamcash hits, but Derek gets forced out. Two outs. The kids chant, "Two out rally! Hit it up the Alley."

Sosa smacks the ball to the outfield and scores Jack and Wamcash. We're now down 3–5 and Jason earns a walk, so we have runners on first and second. Marty is up. Reminding the hitting coach of his role, Harry yells to Nino, "This is big!" Marty earns a walk.

After hearing me say, "Nice pitch," when the ball goes right down the middle but the bat doesn't move, a dad comes to me with a disapproving look. "The rule is they can't swing until they have a strike," he says. In understanding he didn't agree with this, I assure him I'm sure there's a method to Harry's madness, but he doesn't appear convinced. With Marty's walk, the bases are loaded; Stefon walks, we're at 4–5. Jason steals home, and the score is tied. I feel like I may have an accident (did I mention my weak bladder?), and the pitcher is visibly frustrated, throwing dirt. Soon we're up 6–5.

It's the bottom of the fourth. Mac strikes out the first batter. The second batter grounds out, and the next batter pops up between Wamcash and Sosa. Neither calls it, so the ball drops to the ground. The next batter hits a ball that takes a legitimate bad hop, and the opposing team scores. After a couple of errors, they lead, 6–7.

My family has decided to take the lead in bankrolling Luis's snacks, so I can take notes. My stomach is in knots, but I'm drinking a cup of coffee in the blazing sun, sweating.

Top of the fifth—we need to score one to tie and a couple of more if we have any hope against this team. Jacob is hit by a pitch and gets to first base. To make matters worse; he's caught stealing at second, so they get one quick out. Eddie strikes out—two quick outs—and then D-Rod strikes out.

At the bottom of the fifth, Mariano is pitching and looks good. He strikes out the first batter and walks the second. Then a ground out and another strike ends the inning.

The top of the sixth is where details get fuzzy. I'm dizzy from the sun, the hunger, the hot coffee, and going up and down bleacher chairs; I think I'm going to pass out. My notes are a little hard to decipher; it seems Jack hits to the shortstop and gets out. Derek, my superstar who has figured out his family is in the bleachers and poses every time he takes a practice swing, earns a desperate walk, and steals to second. Wamcash hits a single past right field and gets to first. I swear I'm waiting for Derek to score, but Harry (wisely) keeps him at third. (He tells me later on he wasn't going to send a kid home only to get tagged out again and knew his hitters were coming up to bat.) Sosa hits a triple over the third-base line, and Derek scores the tying run (redemption!). Wamcash scores as well, so we are leading 8–7. Jason hits up the middle and scores Sosa.

The umpire walks over to Coach Nino, who, after the reminder from Harry, is stopping the game, calling time, when a batter is up. The kids, I tell you, look confused. From what I can tell, Mac is out, and they are one out away from getting out of this mess and scoring in their last at bat. But it doesn't end. Remember, Harry told the team there were eighteen outs. Jason steals home again, Edgar walks, and Marty scores someone. By the time the inning is over, we are up 11–7. A four-run cushion (we hope) is enough for Wamcash to take us to the promised land in Baseball heaven!

It's the bottom of the sixth; Wamcash walks the first batter. D-Rod in the dugout starts packing his things, prompting Harry and John to yell that the game is not over but he can leave early if he wants to. Nerves are rattled. My mom and two other grandmas are standing and hanging on the fence. I plead to my steady sidekick and fellow mom, Terry, "Could it be—you think we can win?" She assures me she has a good feeling this time. He gets a strikeout, and I'm whispering, "Two more." There's a pop out to the infield, but no one catches it, and the runner gets to second.

Harry calls time, goes to the mound, and gives the team a pep talk. The next batter's up, and an error by our second baseman allows the run to score. They're gaining; the scoreboard reads 11–8. According to Harry, the umpire started "squeezing home plate," and it was hard to get a called strike. Finally, there's a called strike three with the batter looking; the kids go nuts and run on top of catcher Jason with the game ball.

I go blank; the thought of actually winning a championship game is numbing. I'm hugging a lot of moms, and all we're saying is *"Finally!"* Kisses, hugs, yells, and smiles are rampant. We go to center field, where the kids will receive their trophies. But first they huddle at second for their usual end-of-game cheer. Coach Alan calls all the parents out and asks one of us to end the game with a cheer. I quickly volunteer and yell something like, "We're proud of you and have sat through all these games and one-two-three, Tayneck!" (Sorry, I have nothing prepared.) The kids get their trophies, and I get busy setting up the pizza order for the end-of-year party. We have a toast, and the coaches and parents give speeches. I want to remind the doubting dad there is a method to Harry's madness, which worked, but I keep my mouth shut—still dizzy.

I hug every mom (including mine, which was priceless) and I run to the car, get my video camera, and start to record the pandemonium. "Scary Halloween

Eve" may not be an appropriate title for a story about winning, but the notion comes to me while I capture the celebration. The kids run to the trunk of a dad's car, where they find a stash of soda. Shaking and opening the cans, they spray soda all over each other. (Hey, they can't do beer.)

I'm gingerly walking on the field (hoping not to get splashed), and I hear Wamcash saying, "It was scary." So, being the investigative reporter I am, I ask, "What was scary?" And he speaks as any youth would. "This was scary; you know, I'm the closer in a championship game, and it's scary!"

"It was scary, but you did it," I tell him.

All he says is, "Yeah." He slaps me five, but the look is not convincing.

I thought of the semifinals when Harry was yelling at Wamcash to "just throw strikes" and Coach John was arriving in time to get in his face, and I conceded the pressure the kids must feel is unbelievable. The testament to them facing their fears—getting up to the batter's box to bat (despite myriads of coaches yelling at them) or onto the mound to pitch—is commendable.

Suffice it to say, on that beautiful Sunday in October, the official end of daylight savings time was also the end of us going to the big dance and coming up short. The kids did it in fine fashion (notwithstanding several errors or bad hops that probably erased a couple of years off Harry's life expectancy).

A most touching moment, however, happened outside the trophy area. I saw Harry writing the score and date on the game ball, while John gave his speech. I wondered who Harry planned to give the ball to, and I figured it must be me because I baked forty-eight cupcakes, coordinated a pizza party, and dealt with the stress of being the manager's wife for forty-eight games. It wasn't me; he gave it to a player's grandma. She was calmly smiling during the game when the rest of us were in the yelling frenzy. I realized he's not the coldhearted bum I sometimes believe him to be but a sensitive human being. I heard the cell phone message: "I wanted to let you know you made my mother-in-law's day. She cried, said she was proud of the team, and was touched she got the game ball."

It's not about winning or losing, but how you played the game . . . the game of life and humanity. Yeah, it felt fantastic that we won. We deserved it, but at the end of the day, it's what you do with others that count. I'm a firm believer in keeping my side of the street clean, and I try. I yell at Luis and Derek and argue until I'm out of saliva with Harry, but by day's end, they know I love them more than life, and I assure them I'm dancing as fast as I can in my quest to be a better human who gets worked up over youth baseball games. I'm not a Supreme Court justice but a baseball-loving mom who attends and cheers at games. I've gotta believe I'm a winner. I know the 9Us are and can finally say that with proof! Luis summed it up best when he said he wanted to cry, realizing, "Sometimes you cry when you're sad, but you can cry when you're happy, right?"

The 2005 season was a success, capped off by winning game forty-eight with a record of 41–6–1. Of the six losses, four were in championship games. Despite expected differences of opinions inherent in playing forty-eight games through three seasons, with second-guessing, wins, losses, errors, and hurt feelings, it took the forty-eighth game of playing hard, coaching, and cheering for 18 outs to ultimately win. The win was significant in so many ways; it was the culmination of teamwork and trust in what the manager was trying to accomplish. The board was happy, the local paper was provided with a picture of the championship team (with thirteen players and eight dads/coaches!), and my "A Great Season 2005" cupcakes were photographed and pictured in the league website. The parents in all probability saw firsthand that Harry had a sense of what he was doing. There were tears of joy from a little boy who questioned whether it was okay to cry because he was happy. The championship victory was proof this was a town team to be reckoned with, and we were declared the pride of Tayneck. Managing did wonders for Harry—it forced him to open his protected heart and make room for the constellation of boys, coaches, and parents who drove him nuts but, at day's end, made him smile. The memories and bonds forged were priceless. It took forty-eight games and a championship to realize that winning baseball trophies is just the icing on the cupcake!

SPRING 2006-9U

What Time Is It?! Resuming with Roxbury

AFTER THE CHAMPIONSHIP WIN, THE winter was busy with discussions about what the kids would do when the season resumed. We had matching uniforms, cleats, and bags to order and tournaments to enlist in, and another player, Isaac, was joining the fun. We attempted fundraising because, with the planned schedule (which included, for the first time, an opportunity to play outside of New Jersey) we wanted to be ready. We coined the phrase "Tayneck ... what the heck," and it soon became a part of our regular cheer—"One-two-three, Tayneck ... what the heck!" We ordered T-shirts to match. The kids also started a cheer; before every game, they'd get in a circle and yell, *"What time is it?! Game time!"*

For the spring season, we would play in the Marra tournament. The winner would represent New Jersey in the nationals in Oklahoma. The competition would be tougher, since we'd be playing "club" teams, some that had players we'd faced in the past. Club teams consist of various players who do not have to be from the same area and are more competitive, as the managers are not limited to one town area from which to select their players.

Our first game in the tournament is against the club team Roxbury Rangers. Jack is the starting pitcher, and he starts with an immediate groundout to first and strikes out batter number two. Roxbury's third batter is big (looks at least thirteen) and slams the ball to the outfield for an in-the-park home run; it's 0–I. Jack walks the next batter, who steals second despite a nice throw from catcher Stefon to second baseman Derek. And then another walk has kids on first and second. Thankfully, the Rangers' next batter hits the ball to the pitcher, and he's out. The top of the first inning ends.

Jack walks and then steals second and third. Derek strikes out, and up is Wamcash. After a wild pitch, Jack steals home, evening the score at 1–1, and Wamcash walks. Sosa hits a shot to the outfield that leaves everyone's eyes wide open. Wamcash scores, and Sosa stops at third. Another wild pitch, and then Jason strikes out. But Sosa scores. Stefon earns a walk but gets caught trying to steal second. At the end of the first inning, the score is 3–1.

Jack is still pitching at the top of the second. In the scorer's box, I'm gossiping, so I'm not quite sure what happens, except I know Roxbury's runner has stolen home. I see our shortstop run to try to tag a kid, but the umpire calls him safe. The shortstop is holding the ball, and I hear Derek yelling, "C'mon, second!" Complete chaos takes hold of the field. Another kid tries stealing home, but this time Jack gets him out, and the score is 3–2. The big kid hits another shot to the outfield, and the score is 3–4. Another hit to the outfielder, who throws it wildly to Derek. Jack is still holding the ball in the air, trying to run the runner down, and Harry yells, "Stop wasting so much energy doing that!" The score is 3–6.

At the bottom of the second, the big kid is pitching for Roxbury and pitching fast. Edgar and Jacob strike out, and Stan is up and on a full count. He hits to the third baseman and gets to first base. Eddie strikes out, and we're still losing 3–6.

Harry puts Jason in to pitch, and he strikes out the first two up to bat. The third batter hits a pop-up to Derek, who yells, "*I got it!*" But he drops it. My heart sinks and I feel for my kid, who can't stay still while at second base. Derek catches my eye coming to the dugout, and I provide a look of love and support. One mom starts chanting, "Love knowingness, love bliss," and I silently chant along with her. The inning's over, and the error did not result in a run. Whew!

It's the bottom of the third. Their pitcher can't pitch anymore; league rules say each pitcher can only pitch two innings. D-Rod walks, and Nathan (new to the team) strikes out. Jack walks but D-Rod doesn't know he has to run, and Harry is popping a jugular telling him to run to second. Derek hits to third base, and the Rangers' third baseman drops the ball. The bases are loaded for Wamcash. He walks, and a run scores, bringing us to 4–6. Sosa measures his bat with the home plate, hits to the outfield, and Jack and Derek score. Sosa stops at third. Wamcash makes a run for the home plate but runs into the catcher (the rule is you have to slide and avoid contact with the catcher) and is called out. One of the moms hears the umpire say he's throwing Wamcash out, and the coaches go wild. Jason hits a blooper to the pitcher, and he's out. The score is tied at 6–6.

We're at the top of the fourth. What will we do without Wamcash? Coach John pays the umpire his fee in the middle of the game, and it amusingly appears as if he's paying the umpire off, since we see Wamcash up! (John didn't pay him off; the umpire explains that he was simply calling Wamcash out at the plate, with a warning, not out of the game.) Stefon pitches, and the first batter hits to shortstop Sosa and is out. The second kid hits to the pitcher, and he's out too. The third walks and steals second. The last batter strikes out, and the score remains 6–6.

In the bottom of the fourth, Stefon walks, Jason hits, and Jacob walks, but Stan strikes out. After two more outs, the score is still tied at 6–6. Derek and Jack are fighting. Jack yells, "Stop running my life!" because Derek told him to put a helmet on.

Stefon strikes the first batter out at the top of the fifth. Not knowing he's struck out, the kid stands there. Stefon walks the next batter but strikes out the second, and there are two outs. Big Galoopa (now playing on this team) hits a home run, and the score is 6–8. The next batter hits to second, and (thankfully) Derek catches it; the first half of the inning is over.

In the bottom fifth, their pitcher is wild; he throws hard but not accurately. Our first batter earns a walk, and D-Rod gets hit with the pitch and runs slowly to the base. Harry and I steal glances, and we both sigh a collective "whew" when he gets there. Nathan earns a walk, and the coaches start fighting about the "tarp rule"—whether or not you can steal home when the ball goes underneath the tarp. Jack strikes out, Derek walks, and the bases are loaded for Wamcash, who hits and scores D-Rod. The bases are loaded again, and Sosa's up. He hits another base-clearing triple, and the score's 10–8. Jason hits a double (12–8), Stefon strikes out, Jason steals home, and we end the inning up 13–8.

At the top of the sixth, Sosa's pitching. The batter hits a pop-up to Marty at third, who drops it. The next batter hits to first, and he's out. Another hit goes to our third baseman. He throws it slowly to first base, and the runner beats the throw; they score. It's 13–9. A strikeout makes two outs. A wild throw from Sosa, and a runner steals home, bringing the score to 13–10. The last batter strikes out, and the game is over. We win 13–10.

Robbing the Bandits and More?

BEAUTIFUL, SUNNY BASEBALL WEATHER AND bleachers full of family and visitors—a mom proclaimed, "It's baseball time, and we're all here." We passed a bag of sunflower seeds around. We would be playing another club team, the Bandits, a group of bigger, lankier kids, who, during warm-up, looked good. Coach Alan saw me biting my nails and asked if I was nervous. I lied and said, "No."

Game time is different from practice; the umpire, the crowds, the coaches yelling, and the parents cheering all make for a pressure situation. I love that about baseball; there's no Michael Jordan to give the ball to to win the game. It's about the batter and the pitcher and the guys behind the pitcher backing him (or not).

My family members who'd gathered were impressed with the caliber of play, and an occasional "aah," or "ooh," or "wow" was voiced. My cousin asked me during the spitting of sunflower seeds how I write my stories, and I pointed to my brain, saying, "I keep it there, and it flows."

The game is scheduled for 4:00 p.m., but the umpire is late (dinner is prepared already, thankfully). Jason is scheduled to pitch and looks good; he's an athlete through and through and is pitching hard and, importantly, pitching strikes, prompting "aahs," "oohs," and "wows" from my family.

A line drive, which Derek dramatically dives for but misses, goes past second base, and at the end of the inning the Bandits are leading 0–I. Derek and Marty walk, and Jason hits, scoring them both. Sosa's up, and it appears he's pressing; he wants to hit the ball and hit it hard but keeps striking out.

His dad explains he can't hit "slow pitches," only fast (what?). He walks to the dugout with his head down. Stefon and then Edgar are up, and by end of the inning, we're leading 3–1.

Our pitching shuts them down. We score more, and Eddie gets hit on the back. We're aghast at the sound of the hit, and he is taken to the dugout. I tell my cousin Rachel, who's a nurse, to go check on him, of course checking with Harry first. She tells me when she gets back pretty sheepishly that the coach with the white shirt abruptly said, "Eddie is okay," when she went to check. She said there was a lot of testosterone that couldn't handle her estrogen meddling in.

I leave when we're leading 8–2, and by the time I return forty-five minutes later, we're up 13–2. Eddie gets hit again, this time on the other side, and he's rolling around in the dirt. Rachel doesn't bother to check on him—she learned her lesson—but this time he's crying and sits down. Eddie is considered a pretty hard pitcher but is erratic and not used as much. Harry tells me later that a parent asked him, "Why don't you put Eddie in so he can hit one of their kids?" And Harry immediately replied, "I don't play that way."

It's the top of the sixth, and Stefon is pitching in place of the first pitcher, who threw two innings and is now sitting. A couple of errors result in the Bandits scoring some runs, and the score is 13–6.

At about 6:30, stomachs are grumbling, and Stefon is throwing balls. Harry yells, "Throw strikes; let's get out of here!" After some hits, Stefon strikes out the last batter, and the game is over, with a final score of 13–6. I leave, and Harry, along with some of the dads/coaches, stays to clean up.

Harry had been trying to tell me the game is ruined by parents, but my Pollyanna view didn't allow me to believe it. A parent approached Harry after the game and said he wanted to know what to say in the event his son asked him why he was taken out and did not get to play the full game. I was astonished when Harry told me about the situation. How could a parent be so willing to question the manager of a team that has been doing well? I shouted, "Get outta here!" He received no "aahs," "oohs," or "wows" from me.

Harry emphatically replied, "Is this *your* concern or your son's concern?" To this, the parent responded that he needed an answer "in case he asks, since he loves baseball so much." (Which of these kids doesn't love baseball?) Harry told him he didn't have to answer this question and if he wanted to take his kid elsewhere he could. The exchange happened within earshot of another dad who had similar "concerns" regarding his son's playing/pitching time the previous year. Despite the fact that his son was batting third and played the infield, this father questioned whether Harry had his kid "on ice." Harry ended the conversation by stating that he refused to deal with this nonsense this year.

This little "talk" prompted Harry to hold *his* meeting with the players (no parents and no other coaches) so he could talk to the kids about what matters to *them*.

The concern put a damper on the win and, in hindsight, seemed to be the beginning of a trend that was developing among parents. Even when a *team* came together to win, parents questioned the actions of those responsible. The Bandits may have gotten robbed of the game, but it was appearing as if it was Harry's integrity that was robbed when a parent questioned a decision to rest a pitcher.

Harry wondered whether it was time to take the advice of a coach who suggested, "Forget the parents" (a phrase we silently coined FTP). The attention should be directed on the kids. Isn't that who the "aahs," "oohs," and "wows" are supposed to be for?

Tent People: The Emergence of Family

AFTER A YEAR OF BASEBALL and a spring during which my weekends consisted of more games, my family started questioning my absence. With fifteen teammates and siblings playing and families gathering, it was okay to take a sabbatical.

The 9Us next embarked on the Hackensack Memorial Day Tournament. We were to play the Rangers, Alexander, and Fairfield to make it to the championship game against the green monster known (in my mind) as Watson.

The night before the tournament, Derek overheard Harry telling me he was going to put Derek in left field. Derek, the drama king, was devastated and yelled, "Dad is treating me like a piece of rock because he never plays me at second base in a tournament!" Harry reminded him of the catch made in the outfield during the fall championship game and of an arm that could get balls into the infield quickly, but Derek was sad. Harry, who had been second-guessed by parents, was now being second-guessed by his player (!) and must have threatened to quit coaching because Derek wrote him a note:

> *Dear Dad,*
>
> *Please don't be your last year coaching me [sic] because you are a great dad and coach and please during the tournament please put me at second base and not the outfield.*
>
> *By: Derek your son*

Harry struggled with diverting from batting the entire lineup and thought of playing only nine kids to move the lineup quickly. This didn't result in good feelings; those who played were happy; those who didn't weren't. It was tense for Harry to tell the families of kids, some of whom had been with us since the beginning, that their kids would sit in the dugout. Harry started getting precautionary texts asking questions like, "Is my son going to play?" Others, from parents whose kids were sitting, editorialized as to why this particular kid in the lineup should be replaced. Managing was getting difficult, but he forged ahead.

We started Friday night against our new nemesis, Roxbury. In the all-star spring tournament, our record against Roxbury was one win and one loss. The tournament organizers placed us in pool B, along with three other good teams, including Watson and Roxbury and the Milford Wolfpacks. The managers complained that including the three best teams in the same pool was unfair, so the tournament organizers changed the semifinal game to allow the opportunity for the two best teams to emerge, and they did.

Jason's mom brought a tent to shade the spectators from the heat of the unusually hot weekend. Walking back from the bathroom, I was greeted by the comical sight of over twenty people huddling and cheering under an eight-foot-by-eight-foot tent. We were affectionately coined the "tent people."

From under this tent, I kept my own scorebook filled with statistics. Along with making Coach John paranoid—"You keeping score too?"—I figured I would do something worthwhile. My idea was that my scorebook would be a resource for Harry to turn to at home, since Coach John (scorekeeper extraordinaire who taught me well) kept the book. But more importantly, I would be able to prove Harry wrong. Harry's ability to replay a game in his head like it had just happened never failed to amaze me. I couldn't believe he could truly remember the pitch count, strikeouts, and location where each ball was hit, so like any good wife, I set out to prove my spouse wrong and started keeping my own book. Suffice it to say, Harry wasn't wrong. Plays of the game are embedded in his head like security codes in the mind of a CIA director. Little did I know, this was the beginning of my transition from bleacher to dugout.

We played Fairfield in the semifinal game and jumped to a 2–0 lead early. But in the bottom of the second, the leadoff batter hit a home run. Fairfield scored four more and took a 2–5 lead. In the top of the third, we had a two-run rally and were down 4–5. During the top of the sixth, we tied the game 6–6 and played extra innings. Thankfully, we got some cushion with three more runs. Then came the bottom of the seventh. Fairfield fought back and had the tying run at the plate, but our defense stopped any attempt at taking the game away from them. We won!

The championship game against another of our rivals, Watson, was to start after a short break, so the moms ushered the kids under the tent to give them fruit, chips, and water and to fan them. With the amount of care extended to all the boys, I felt like I was with family. Coach Harry and John asked the boys if this was all they wanted, to which they replied no. They wanted Watson. We had first encountered Coach Beck and his mighty team the previous year. They beat us by executing bunts, which our team wasn't prepared to field. Soon thereafter, bunting was on the agenda. Harry reminded them—eighteen outs; play all eighteen outs.

I guess the adrenaline from having defeated Fairfield in extra innings allowed the boys to jump to a 3–1 lead in the second inning. Then Watson ambushed our fatigued players and, thanks to hits and various team errors, went up 3–9.

In the top of the sixth, the kids fought back, decreasing the lead of 7–11. We exploded for six more runs to take a 13–11 lead. Then Watson made a pitching change. Unfortunately, Tayneck couldn't capitalize on the momentum and get more runs.

Wamcash came in after Watson had put the first two runners on base and struck out his first batter. The next batter bunted the ball, which was mistakenly thrown to right field by Wamcash, allowing them to score and taking the score to 13–12. Wamcash struck out the next batter, and with two outs, it looked like the curse of the Bambino was over.

Unfortunately, the catcher overthrew the ball to the pitcher, and Watson sent their runner home! The score was tied. The next batter ran the count up to 3–2 and then hit over the right fielder's head. Watson won.

Parents gave the kids a standing ovation, having watched great games against two fierce competitors and coaches. After Watson beat us, Derek called the inability to beat Watson the "second curse of the Bambino."

We added new lingo to our team. Along with "tent people" we also cheered, "buen ojo" (our Spanish version of "good eye"). The siblings (not players) cried when the game was over, and Coach John opened his home (the "Copley cabana") to us for some fun. The point is we came together, like family, and while not holding the championship trophy, we emerged better for it.

This team was becoming, as Coach Alan called them, "a band of brothers." And while the players were not genetically linked, there was no keeping them (or their families) from each other. Baseball games were just a venue to gather, cheer, laugh, watch, and win. I warned my family I would be missing in action but would make it a point to be around for Thanksgiving. There wouldn't be any baseball in November . . . would there?

SUMMER AND FALL
2006-9U

Mucho Games and Hasty Decisions

THE AMOUNT OF GAMES PLAYED was increasing, and I did not have time to write detailed stories. Between June and mid-July, the team had thirty games scheduled in three different tournaments. We then had play-offs in the NJABC Tournament, the Preston Tournament, and the Bainbridge Tournament—all within a week's time. I couldn't quite place it, but something felt as if the team was different. The kids showing up were not the same kids I'd watched for the past couple of years. Was it too much baseball?

Harry was not concerned. He thought playing fifteen kids was the anchor bringing this ship down.

Hillsdale came to play. Unable to stomach the Hillsdale coach talking to every player, during every single play and every single pitch, I left the scorer's booth and begged my friend to take over. We were losing 5–14, so you can imagine the testosterone from his mouth.

In the bottom of the sixth, Luis told me he wasn't feeling well and wanted to go home. He was warm, so I left, thinking the game was over. We got home; Luis got cleaned up, got some medicine, laid on the couch, and fell asleep. A reliable mom called to give me an update, letting me know that, with two outs, we scored six, and the score was 11–14 before it was all over. We lost but fought back.

We headed back to Bainbridge for our fourth game of the tournament. (We'd played three over the weekend and had the group stay at a hotel, and we'd left with an impressive 3–0 record.) We were scheduled to play Greenburgh, who was also 3–0, so the importance of the game was obvious; somebody was going to come out the top seed for the play-offs. I did my research and saw that this team was creaming the other teams by obnoxious scores, so my nerves were jangled. We left at 8:30 a.m. and arrived ready for warm-ups before our 10:30 start. Something was different about this Greenburgh team; theirs did not look like the other players we had opposed—they looked really, really good. I realized we were up for a challenge, which is not bad.

Edgar pitched. After a shaky first inning, during which our kids made errors—were they intimidated by the size and skills of the other team?—Greenburgh scored and was leading 0–3. We scored two in the top of the second inning by getting on base and then stealing second; the score was 2–3. Greenburgh ended up getting one more run, but following some great defensive catches by Stefon, Jack, and Derek, that's all they did.

Our pitching was phenomenal, as was theirs, but we lost 2–4. We left proud of the way we'd played against the obviously better qualified team, and we were satisfied with the final score (given the whippings Greenburgh had been giving other teams). The other families caravanned back home, but my clan, along with Coach John's, stayed for lunch.

Harry talked to the tournament director for, I assumed, scheduling purposes. Little did I know.

I cleaned my house and cooked dinner before the next game at 6:00 p.m. On our way to the field, Harry received a call from the Bainbridge tournament director. He was advised the team that beat us was an "illegal team." Club and town teams are different, and when we played against club teams, as a strictly town team, it was impressive. This tournament was strictly for town teams, and Greenburgh had signed up not only with only three town players but with older kids, which was prohibited. The team was disqualified, and we were given a forfeited win.

We were now 4–0 in the tournament and top seed for the play-offs. Harry assembled the parents to tell them, and everyone let out a collective, "I knew it." Greenburgh didn't look like a town nine-year-old team.

Despite a tornado watch, we drove fifteen miles to play our last regular season game. We batted fifteen. I took my time arriving because I figured the game was going to be cancelled. We arrived, and I exchanged my wet sneakers for a pair of sandals. PMS was kicking in—I didn't want to hear these moms. The kids were yelling, "We are Tayneck, mighty, mighty Tayneck!" I told them to stop yelling. Hearing them sing the song in whispers was hysterical.

I asked Terry if I sounded a bit harsh, and she politely said, "Just a bit." (She is the epitome of a graceful Southern woman.) To enable the kids to yell, I walked away from the bleachers.

We're winning 3–1. Wamcash is pitching. An error by the catcher, who tries to pick off the runner at third base and throws the ball away, results in our opponent tying the game. Harry tells Wamcash to "just pitch." I'm busy trying to find ice in a hot, humid, bug-filled baseball field because Luis was hit in the face with a bat while struggling with another sibling who wanted it. Luis doesn't want to use the ice but the eye is swelling. I convince him to do it, and he sits with the two cubes of ice we found near his face. Ramsey scores again, and they're leading 3–4.

At the top of the sixth, we have the bottom of the lineup up to bat, and the first two strike out. The next kid hits, steals second, and Derek is up. He gets a full count, and I can't watch. Harry tells him to "protect" and reminds him the pitch has to be "perfect." I don't watch; all I hear is *smack!* Turns out the little dynamo gets a double. Harry holds the runner at third, as he's been burned too many times sending kids home. The next kid strikes out, and we lose.

After the loss, Harry addressed the parents, who were packing up lawn chairs, in as firm and emotionless a tone as he could: he would be "shrinking" the lineup because now "real baseball" would start with the play-offs. He was going to play nine, meaning at least six were going to sit.

When he went to bed and said his prayers, Derek thanked God for a good day, that we got home safe, and "that I got a double even though I was freakishly nervous while I was up there." I laughed. The kid had me fooled. I was thinking he was okay, when in fact he was "freakishly nervous" but came through. Although I was sure they thought it, parents couldn't accuse Harry of playing Derek because he was his son.

I was nervous about the prospect of all the upcoming games—a mother's worry for her son who was freakishly nervous when he was batting and the pressure of not one but several games. Whatever happened would be God's will, and in the end, maybe he was listening to Derek. Was Oklahoma in our cards? Only God knew. No wonder *I* was freakishly nervous!

Zapping Out the Fun

We were scheduled to face Watson early Saturday morning. Watson had beaten us twice in two separate championship games. Normally carefree and loose, Harry was really intense and stressed-out. He left early so he could get the dugout he wanted (and possibly to meditate).

We didn't have the blue tent but a tarp to shield some of the blazing sun.

Watson arrived with their fancy scoreboard and a fashionable green tent that matched their green uniforms. And the game was hyped. The intensity of that game was like no other. As expected, it was a classic competition and one of the unfortunate instances where I did *not* have my notes.

In an exciting, nail-biting, impressive 5–4 victory, with Wamcash on the mound and Sonny incessantly cheering the boys on, Tayneck won, prompting kids, parents, and coaches to kick up their heels (literally) and cheer their heads off. Our resident photographer/videographer, Coach Alan (aka Spielberg), made a team video, which my words couldn't replicate. In Derek's immortal words, "The second curse of the Bambino is over!" I literally peed on my pants from a weakened bladder while I was jumping for joy. I was embarrassed, mortified, and shocked—not that we won but that I let my problem get to this.

The women stated that they were going to get lunch for the boys. I told Harry I had to go home to change because I was a mess. He looked at me as if I wanted this to happen. I grabbed Luis and started the drive back home but saw a store and purchased a fresh pair of shorts. I headed back, and although it had been nearly forty-five minutes, the moms were not back. They finally arrived but not before Mayfield, big bad Mayfield, arrived with their bunch of parents and tent and food.

The Mayfield game was an eye-opener. These kids hit, and with the small fence and big barreled bats, home runs were easy. We got one run and stayed there. They scored a lot and, but for a running play by Stan, who got caught between first and second base with their first baseman running ever so slowly behind him, we got to score another two but lost.

Given the scenario—Tayneck beat Watson and Mayfield beat Tayneck—Watson is to play Mayfield. Watson beat Mayfield, and because it's double elimination, the director scheduled a meeting Sunday night (we were assembled for Coach John's birthday) to put the names of the teams in a hat. Whatever name got chosen would go to the championship game, and the other two teams had to battle it out. Was it the birthday wish for Coach John? Who knows, but we were picked! Could it be we'd be going to Oklahoma?

Mayfield and Watson were scheduled to play, and Harry went to watch. Watson was beating Mayfield by a couple of runs until Mayfield hit a grand slam to win the game. The championship game would be Mayfield versus Tayneck.

This time, Watson was stunned! Parents were pumped, and e-mails exclaiming the energy and excitement were sent. The board of directors wanted to come and watch. We took Derek out of summer camp early and headed to the game.

Harry left for the field early to get to the dugout, meditate, plan, plot, and think. And the caravan of cars followed him. We had the boom box playing stadium jams, all the kids had eye black, Mayfield had their cheerleader, and I was not able to stomach anything.

We started the game leading 1–0 with good base running and a stealing frenzy. Mayfield scored two in the bottom of the sixth. After a couple of home runs, the final score was 2–13. We got our butts kicked. Harry was starting to feel the pressure. I didn't know if it was just families whose mojo and karma had soured. Maybe it was me; it felt as if I was the one living my life through the eyes of my son, but the fact that we were not going to Oklahoma really bugged me. After the game, I sat back and saw that the boys took it hard (Luis was teary-eyed in the car). Harry was sad and couldn't believe the dream was over.

However, as the second-seeded team, we were asked if we wanted to go to Oklahoma. Harry told me, "the fun got zapped," and reminded me that a parent e-mailed the entire team, questioning his decision to only bat nine, which left a bad taste in our mouths. It stunned Harry and added to the bad feeling. I told him he couldn't give up on the Oklahoma dream. But when we got home, Harry turned down the request to go as the second seed. I didn't understand the haste in his decision. Was it the disappointment? The comments from the parents? I was upset once I found out Watson took our place. Harry felt worse.

We played the following day in the Preston championship and lost in the bottom of the sixth by a score of 6–7. Mojo was bad—real bad. The deed was done. We had one more tournament to go. Let's see what Bainbridge holds. My son is not upset about Oklahoma. Why was I?

Bainbridge Tournament: Who Needs Oklahoma?

AFTER THE DEVASTATING LOSS AGAINST Mayfield, we played a tournament in Bainbridge. While it wasn't Oklahoma, this was the 9U travel team's first official travel excursion. It was a four-game minimum tournament, and after much planning, Harry was able to get three games on the weekend, which allowed us to stay at the Courtyard Marriot for two nights. We had two games scheduled for Saturday and one for Sunday. Harry thought it would be a nice experience (and a test run for our September tournament in Maryland) to stay at a hotel Friday night, sleep over, and get to the field for the early Saturday morning game. Our first game would be against Bainbridge.

We were missing three kids, who were on vacation, and ten of the twelve who would play arrived Friday night. We checked into our hotel room, and the kids made it to the pool quickly. The dads stayed to watch the kids, and the moms shopped for essentials for the kids. We returned, and the men went out to check out the field. That left me to organize dinner for ten players, their siblings, and the remaining family members. I settled on pizza plus a couple of salads and dinner in the hotel lobby as the kids watched wrestling. The men came back, the other families arrived, and we stayed in the hotel lobby talking and joking. We established a 10:30 curfew for the kids. The men stayed downstairs drinking and looked at me like I was insane when I told them *their* curfew was 11:00 p.m.

On Saturday morning, Harry rode to the field with another coach; he won the coin toss, and we were the home team. Bainbridge had a couple of kids that were tall, and I overheard someone say they were ten-year-olds playing nine-year-old baseball. (Remember, some of our kids were still eight!) We always said it wasn't the age of the kid that mattered but the heart attached to it. Coach Sonny always reminded the boys "it's not the size of the dog in the fight but the size of the fight in the dog" As Coach John would say, "The bigger they are, the harder they fall."

Jason is pitching but struggling and starts off with two walks. Bainbridge's third batter hits a shot to the outfield, and they have a 0–3 lead.

We bat in the bottom of the first, and while they have a big, lanky kid pitching, he's not that powerful. Our first two batters walk, and Sosa and Stefon both hit, bringing the score to 2–3.

At the top of the second, Bainbridge's first batter strikes out. Sosa gets another out, but Bainbridge scores, and it's 2–4. We bat the bottom of the second and score three, jumping to a 5–4 lead.

In the top of the third, Eddie's pitching and gets two strikeouts. Stan is full of cheers and yells, "It's a new batter, same plan!" Eddie hits a batter, and a controversial play ensues—a runner going to third gets hit by the ball, which would make him out. Bainbridge claims that the kid wasn't hit, but you heard it and saw the kid limping. Coach John yells to the umpire, "Ask him how his foot is!" And the umpire calls the kid out, but not before they've scored two and now lead 5–6. One of their coaches has this annoying habit of reminding them they "won an inning" (as in a boxing match) by matching up our scores. In actuality, they won a lot of the innings.

We bat in the bottom of the third. Stefon strikes out, Jason hits to third, and Marty hits. However, we don't score. We lost that inning as well.

Eddie's pitching again at the top of the fourth. A kid gets called safe during a questionable play, and again they score, now leading 5–7.

We bat the bottom of the fourth. The sun is blazing, and Luis is bugging me for snacks. I walk to Harry to try to calm him down. Again Harry ignores me. Mac strikes out. Stan hits but doesn't hustle. And Eddie strikes out.

At the top of the fifth, Eddie strikes out the first kid. The second batter hits a line drive to the outfield and gets a double. Eddie hits another batter. They score again and are leading 5–8.

Bottom of the fifth—it's tight. They get two outs, but Jack scores. Sosa hits a shot over the third basemen's head, and we have runners on first and second. I can't tell you what happened because I'm running back with Luis to the port-o-san, but when I come back, I know we'll end up either tying the game or going up one.

It's the top of the sixth, and Bainbridge is up. Sosa misses a hit to him. Eddie gives up a walk, and Harry talks to him. The runner steals third, and Eddie earns a strikeout. With the bases loaded, Harry brings in Stefon, who gets a strikeout. Now there are two outs. He walks a runner, and they tie the game.

In the bottom of the sixth, Stan hits a blooper that gets overthrown to first base. He gets to second base, and there's a questionable call out for the next batter. We go into extra innings.

They score at the top of the seventh; we have to score in order to win. I don't know what happens because I'm too nervous to write and pissed because my new sneakers are hurting my feet, I don't have my chair, and Luis doesn't stop asking for food. All I have in my notes is "Top 7—scores." I don't know how we did it, but we won the game.

Harry stays at the park to get lunch for the kids. I'm still annoyed because of my feet and sit by myself during lunch. The umpires are telling Harry and John that our kids played well, and everybody (except me) feels good.

We walk to the other field for our second game against North Bridgewater. The kids are pumped, and I'm even more pumped because I see the small size of the kids and hope the game will be an easier one. I'm sitting at the bleachers, and Harry comes over to kiss me, surprising all who witness this rare event. I get rid of the orthotics in my sneakers, which I didn't realize were making my shoes tighter, and wish Harry good luck.

We lose the coin toss, bat first, and immediately score three because of errors. Sosa takes the mound, and North Bridgewater doesn't score.

During the top of the second, we score six from a Stan double, an Edgar blooper, a Jack double and sacrifice by Derek, and a Stefon hit. The kids come back to the dugout up 9–0, and Coach Nino tells them to "mercy" (have a big enough lead by a certain inning to end the game) this team and go back to the pool. I know if I were the opposing coach and heard this, which he probably did because Coach Nino was talking pretty loudly, I would motivate my kids to play, which is what they did. They scored one in the bottom of the second but came back to score four in the bottom of the third, by which time the score was 10–5.

We bat at the top of the fourth and don't score.

In the bottom of the fourth, Harry brings in Marty to pitch, and he gets a strikeout. Then Derek's nice play at second earns two outs immediately.

During the top of the fifth, we score two—12–5.

It's the bottom of the fifth. Harry asks Marty whether his energy's good, and Marty assures him it is. So Harry leaves him in. Jack makes a nice throw out at home, but North Bridgewater still scores two. It's 12–7.

We bat the top of the sixth and North Bridgewater gets three quick outs. Marty continues pitching, and we win 12–7.

The kids ran to the pool. I made dinner arrangements—including a surprise birthday cake for Harry. It was a nice break. The kids swam for several hours, we shared food and cake in the back of the hotel's outdoor lobby, and the boys presented Harry with a plaque with pictures of the team taken during a tournament. In the image on the top of the plaque, the team was assembled—all fifteen kids and six coaches/dads. In the photo at the bottom, the kids were sitting and listening to one of Harry's talks. The plaque read, "Happy Birthday, Coach Harry, from his boys. We love you for all you have done for us." Harry was visibly moved. Harry, Alan, and Dennis smoked cigars; John drank some Goose; Nino swam and threw the kids around; and some of the parents played cards and dominos or talked. It was a phenomenal first-time "travel experience."

On Sunday morning, I left to attend a wedding (solo, as was becoming customary—Harry rarely missed baseball games), as did three players. But the nine who remained played hard to win the third game 11–2. Edgar pitched five innings. While at the wedding in a fancy dress, I silently wished I was at the field in shorts and tight sneakers.

My kids have each other as brothers, but they also have fourteen other players and siblings. Luis and I talked about his favorite people in the world. Mom was number one, Dad number two, and Derek number three. And then Luis started with number four all the way to number nine and listed the names of Derek's teammates. When a six-year-old kid numbers among his favorite people his brother's teammates, there's an impression being made. We had a good thing going, despite the egos that seemed to be surfacing among some of the parents when it came to their boys. The memories of Bainbridge 2006 were the precursor to many great travel excursions.

We were 7–0 in this tournament. The pitchers were phenomenal, the bats were meeting the ball, and the defensive plays were good but for a couple of errors. The parents were rightfully loud in their place under the big blue tent. I reminded myself, *Who needs Oklahoma when we have Bainbridge, New Jersey?*

Neck Pains: The Cal Ripken Experience

THE NOW DIMINISHED TEAM OF twelve players (we lost three kids from the summer team) and their families drove 165 miles to Aberdeen, Maryland, to play baseball. For a baseball psycho mom like me, this was great. I took the day off and took advantage of a spa certificate, enjoying a refreshing massage and facial. The calm I felt dissipated later at a highway rest stop, when I yelled at Luis and Derek, who were riding their "heely" sneakers, falling every couple of seconds, and almost knocking down seniors with walkers.

Many of the parents were arriving late, and unlike in Bainbridge, the lobby at the Aberdeen Holiday Inn was not an accommodating spot for us to hang out and await family arrivals.

The Cal Ripken tournament had a set schedule. The games were to be played at a scheduled time, and each team was scheduled for batting practice in the official batting cages at a specific time. The kids hadn't played for a while. It was imperative to get them to the cages to warm up. I think I needed it more than they did. We were supposed to play at 9:00 a.m. A never-ending rainstorm resulted in delays. After much speculation and the maintenance guys driving around and cleaning the fields, the officials decided to cancel the Saturday games.

We went back to the hotel, the sun emerged, and Harry was annoyed. We ordered pizza for the kids, who were swimming in the cold indoor pool, and talked about driving down to Baltimore to hang out on the pier. The kids showered and changed, some of the parents napped, and a caravan of cars drove to Baltimore, Maryland. We stopped to watch a street show, with Coach John dancing in public, and then took the kids to the ESPN Zone to play video games.

The revised schedule had us playing a game at 8:00 a.m. and another at 3:30 p.m. We were scheduled to play the White Sox from Brooklyn, who looked young. The manager was a woman who impressed me.

We won 16–1. Most people would consider this an impressive victory. For Harry, it was the ending of the tournament for us, and I couldn't understand why. We had allowed one run, he explained. Twenty-four teams were vying for a championship spot, so allowing even one run could spell defeat. There were sure to be some teams that didn't allow any. I was annoyed with his frown and even more so because the run was a result of Derek's error.

We got lunch before the second game, and I recited the stats to Harry. He asked, "How did that run come in?"

Poor, innocent Derek said, "Oh, that was me. The ball was popped up, and I said, 'I got it,' but I didn't. And the guy on third base came home."

Harry exclaimed, "Ohhh, man, that's right," and started talking to Derek about how he missed it.

I retorted that he couldn't blame the entire game on Derek. Wasn't it the pitcher who walked two batters who were on base?! I reminded him that he's very quick to judge and told him to see what happens in game two.

He stayed quiet. Unlike me protecting my young, Harry was honestly explaining the facts.

Next up were the Rockland Raptors. I heard someone in the concession line stating, "Tayneck won 16–1, but it doesn't matter because that was a crappy team," and I got annoyed.

We're the visiting team, so we bat first, and immediately, Jack walks. Derek, the alleged "goat" from game one, smacks a double to the outfield. Sosa strikes out looking, and Wamcash gets a single, scoring Jack and Derek. Jason flies to the third baseman, and Marty gets out. We lead 2–0.

Harry starts Mac, who threw two impressive innings in game one, on the pitcher's mound, and the Raptors score one after Mac walked someone and their cleanup hitter whacked the ball to the outfield, earning a triple. Everyone's jaws drop. This kid is good. At the end of the first inning, the score is 2–1.

During the second inning, we don't score. And when they bat, they do, after errors were made (not by Derek!). It's now 2–3.

Again, we don't score in the top the third, and when they bat, they score, bringing the board to 2–4.

At the top of the fourth, Sosa gets on base. Wamcash whacks a triple, scoring Sosa, and then scores on a hit. The game is tied at 4–4. We hold them in the bottom of the fourth and get to the top of the fifth.

Each game has a two-hour time limit, and I'm keeping track of the time. Sure enough, the Raptors seem to be employing delaying tactics—the Rockland manager takes his time asking questions of the female umpire, who is a bit too friendly with him. During the top of the fifth, we don't score.

Harry brings in Sosa to pitch. Mac did a good job but could only pitch two. At the bottom of the fifth, the score is tied. Sosa gives up a hit. An error by the shortstop and another one by the third baseman result in two runs. The Raptors are leading 4–6, and it's not looking good. Sosa gets a called third strike, and there's one out. They score one more on an error by the shortstop, and we enter the top of the sixth down by 4–7, with Derek coming up to bat first.

Derek gets a hit or earns a walk (my stat-keeping skills are raw) but is on base. Sosa strikes out, Derek steals second, and Wamcash gets a single. Jason strikes out, and Marty walks. Two outs, the bases are loaded, and Stefon's up. He whacks the ball to right field, scoring Derek, Wamcash, and Marty to tie the game! I realize this good roll started when I moved from behind the plate to the first-base sideline, and superstition tells me I have to stay there. Parents and kids are yelling, "Two out rally; hit it up the alley!" And the Rockland pitcher, the kid who hit the triple, is crying! The manager calls time-out to tell him (I would imagine) to calm down.

Even more galling is their coach asking the umpire whether we changed the lineup. Coach John and Harry go crazy. John yells at the umpire, "I'm not even going to justify that question with a response!" and advises that we've had this lineup the whole game. "Move on!" he tells the umpire. "We're not answering that question."

Mac hits, and Stan gets a blooper. The bases are loaded again. Eddie hits a line drive that scores two. At the bottom of the sixth, the score is 9–7. We're able to hold them, and we win.

An official on the phone was watching the game. Harry says the tournament directors had us in contention as a team who could potentially play in the championship game, but we allowed runs and were bumped. Derek doesn't understand and immediately asks, "What time is the championship game?" I have to let him know we aren't in.

The kids headed to the big field, ate hot dogs and fries, and watched the championship game begin.

We left at about 6:30 p.m. to make the long but happy ride home. We didn't win a championship, but we went undefeated and gave teams "neck pains." Coach John pulled up to our car and pointed to his neck, and Derek laughed. I admitted to Harry that he'd been right about the importance of allowing no runs. Derek apologized for the error in the first game, and Harry told him he shows up, cheers everybody, and never gives up. Derek nestled in the chair to sleep, and I swore I saw a smile by that neck.

Fall 2006

AFTER A FALL SEASON DURING which we achieved the best record of 8–1, we played a semifinal against Hartford Blue. As was becoming customary, I was nervous and Harry went to the field unusually loose and carefree. We were the designated home team, and Mac would pitch. The Hartford Blue coach told Harry he would only play nine because a couple of the kids were going to game 7 of the Mets versus St. Louis. Harry said, "Yeah, right," and I wondered if we should have reverted back to playing nine but kept quiet.

Mac allows a single but strikes out the second batter for the first out. The third batter hits a grounder to the shortstop and is out. A wild pitch allows a run to score, and up is Big Galoopa. He comes up to bat, hits to the shortstop and is out. The score is 0–1.

Jack walks and steals second. Derek hits the ball to the second baseman, who gets him out at first. Sosa earns a walk and gets to second. Jack's on third, Sosa's at second, and Wamcash is up. My scorebook shows he had three balls, and I think in some sort of rundown, gets caught because there are three outs, and we didn't score.

Mac is still pitching the top of the second and doing fantastic as he strikes out the side. It would go on that way in the top of their third inning, as they remained scoreless thanks to our defensive plays. A 0–1 game among ten-year-olds (including some nine-year-olds) is impressive.

During the bottom of the second inning, nothing.

At the bottom of the third, Stan pops up to the first baseman and is out, Jacob strikes out, and Eddie hits and is on base. Jack walks, and Derek's up. Occasionally Harry takes Derek to a hitting instructor whom Derek likes. On a recent outing, Derek told me the instructor told him to be "loose as a goose" when batting. I told him I would yell "goose" to remind him. When he's up, I yell, "Goose!" Derek hits past the second baseman. He gets on base with a smile and is responsible for bringing Eddie home to tie the game. Wamcash is up after Sosa walks but strikes out.

Sosa pitches the top of the third and fourth and strikes out two. Combined with defensive plays—a nice catch from third to first base, a high pop-up to Edgar out in left field, and a phenomenal run/chase by Stefon in right field who caught Big Galoopa's bomb—the outs take us to the inning's end.

Our fourth, fifth, and sixth innings are stressful as we put kids on base, but nothing materializes. Jason walks, Marty strikes out, Stefon hits a grounder to the first baseman, Edgar walks, and Mac strikes out looking, for a total of three outs in the fourth.

In the bottom of the fifth, Stan beats out a blooper to first, Jacob gets on base with a hit, and Eddie walks. Bases are loaded again. What happens? Jack and Derek strike out looking, and Sosa strikes out swinging. Three outs with the bases left loaded—not good.

Wamcash pitches the top of the fifth and sixth. In the top five, he strikes out the first two, and the third batter flies to third base.

At the top of the sixth, they single, and then an error by the pitcher allows a runner on base. The third batter grounds out. With one out, the Big Galoopa is up. Harry calls time, goes to the umpire, and asks whether the rules allow for an intentional walk; he's told yes. He signals for the walk, and the kids look pretty professional. The catcher is calling for the balls to be thrown outside, and I worry because the Big Galoopa can hit an outside pitch. The bases are loaded. A female board member, a baseball lover like me, says this is tricky. Their fifth batter pops up the ball to shortstop Sosa, and as the runner starts to leave the base, Sosa catches the ball and tags second base for a *double play!* Coach Alan actually jumps up and down screaming, "Yeah!" The board member says pretty sincerely, "That was a smart play." We got out of a very precarious situation.

We bat the bottom of the sixth with the middle lineup, but strikeouts and ground outs result in extra innings. Given the two-inning pitching rule, Harry decides to bring in Jason, who gets an immediate first out. The second batter grounds to first base. Two outs. The third singles, and Jason walks the ninth batter. With a wild pitch, the coach sends the runner home. The runner is called safe, and the score's 1–2.

We bat last. Stefon grounds from second to first for the first out. Edgar gets a nice hit to the outfield and is on base. Mac gets on base after an error by the right fielder, who caught the ball but then dropped it. Stan strikes out, and Jacob gets hit by the pitcher. The bases are loaded. With two outs, Eddie gets two balls and a strike. He gets a second strike. The spectators are quiet (praying?). The Hartford pitcher throws a beautiful pitch. Eddie watches, and the umpire yells, "Strike three!" Hartford is out of control with excitement.

The kids lined up to shake hands, and the Hartford coach embraced Harry. Harry talked to the team about the final fall game. He told them to hold their heads high but reminded them the team left fourteen runners on base and struck out thirteen times.

We went home and watched the Mets game. I was amused by what I saw. The bottom of the ninth, with runners on base, and a superstar, millionaire major leaguer got a beautiful pitch down the plate but looked at it. How could you get upset at a kid when a major leaguer did the same thing? Harry said baseball was a crazy game because you couldn't rely on one person to do it for you. It was a team effort, and in the end, pitching and defense dominated the game.

WINTER TOURNAMENT
2006-9U

Baseball ... Indoors

WE TOOK THE SHOW ACROSS the George Washington Bridge to the Bronx to compete in a 10U, wood bat indoor tournament. We'd be playing in an indoor dome for a couple of weekends until December leading up to the play-offs, if we made it. Harry mentioned that the manager's meeting was full of machismo, bravado, and testosterone from the managers from the Bronx, Brooklyn, and Washington Heights, among others. Harry worried about baseball overkill.

After dirt and grass fields, the parents were not sure what to expect from this setting, and information was scarce. The parents were told no cleats were allowed (prompting them to run out and buy red and white sneakers because we are a fashionable bunch). Nor could we use aluminum bats (this prompted them to run out and buy wooden bats because we are a dedicated bunch).

I met the team at the dome because I was at my niece's birthday party. I swore Derek would tell me he would miss the game because he enjoyed spending time with his cousin, but instead, it was perfectly fine for us to get to the birthday party with his uniform in the car, eat food and cake, change, and leave at 6:00 p.m. (for an 8:00 p.m. start).

I arrived at the dome at 7:00 p.m. with Derek, Luis, and my nephew, Sean. It was crowded, and two teams seemed to be warming up. Our game was to start at 8:00 p.m., and I knew from looking at the schedule that the other game had started at 6:00 p.m. So I was puzzled by the warming up that was still taking place. Since I knew our caravan was awaiting the arrivals of some latecomers, I decided to find whatever available seats I could and wait. I warned Harry of what I saw.

At 7:30, the posse arrived. Harry immediately confronted the director about the delay, who apologized for the inconvenient, first-day screw-up and assured him we would play as soon as we could.

We sat, listened to a lot of bilingual yelling (with Luis quizzically asking me whether the other team spoke Spanish), and watched a decent game that ended 3–2. We were amused by the uniforms (or lack thereof), specifically those of one team with a grammatically incorrect logo—"We never scared." I wondered whether further attention should be directed to the English language rather than baseball.

The game started at 9:00 p.m. (yes, p.m.), and parents were fired up to cheer, since it had been a couple of weeks since our disturbing loss to Hartford. Coach Alan dared the moms to cheer, but Coach John told him that we would not and were "punks because we were in the Bronx." Our opponent was the GunHill Little League, and one of the kids on the team was my brother-in-law's nephew. I shuddered at his size (double Derek's) and hoped size didn't matter. We hovered over the bunch of people in the first row watching the previous game, and no sooner did they stand up that we jumped into their seats.

We were the home team, so we took the field first, and it was hysterical; we were literally three paces away from centerfielder Marty. This didn't look so hysterical for the fielders who were hearing their parents' "suggestions" (the bunch is obsessive and at times overbearing) about how to stand, when to pose for pictures, or how to throw the ball during warm-ups.

Mac is pitching, and the ball is hitting the glove with a loud *thwup*. That kid can pitch. I suggest to Harry that he should commend Mac on his pitching, but he's cautious because he fears that could lead to a sense of entitlement, as Mac's dad has commented on more than one occasion about playing time. Harry tells me the games are more competitive and he's considering a rotation of the more reliable pitchers. There are no pitching limitations in this tournament.

We score two runs by the bottom of the second, and it's a pretty good defensively played game, with pitchers hitting the strike zone and the defense making the plays.

After Mac pitches three innings, Harry brings in Sosa, another *thwup*-sounding pitcher. The *thwups* are followed by a *phwee* (whistle sound) from Coach Nino, who is also giving him signs as to what to pitch (I did say the bunch is obsessive. From day one, Nino has done whatever he can to exert his knowledge of the game). It's almost like a teapot someone forgot to take off the stove—*phwee* (kid looks up); *phwee* (kid looks up); *phwee* (kid looks up). This drives Harry crazy, so he stays away from Nino and continually reminds Sosa to throw strikes. The dome is a small space, and I guess the *phwee* was getting to Coach John because later Harry would tell me he yelled at Sosa (to Nino's displeasure), "Just throw the ball!"

Noise is a little too much in the cramped space. When our boys cheer, I ask Terry to call her husband, John, to tell them to stop. He looks over and rolls his eyes, which probably means my suggestion is not appreciated.

GunHill is able to score on a throwing error by Jason. By the bottom of the fourth we're winning 2–1, and a mom mentions that some insurance runs would help. No sooner has she spoken the words than the wooden bats come alive. Derek hits, Sosa walks, and I'm not quite sure what Wamcash does. Then Jason hits a line drive home run literally inches above our heads, as we're stationed by centerfield. It's his first home run, and his mom is jumping up and down, Bronx or not (punks who?).

We get more hits and execute great defensive plays. The catcher throws out a kid trying to steal second. Derek makes a backhand catch of a shot to second. We win the game, 7–1, and walk out close to 11:00 p.m. It's a Saturday night, but even the coolest of parents might agree that ending a youth baseball game at 11:00 p.m. is a little extreme.

As the kids and coaches were lining up exchanging "good game," one of their coaches hugged Harry and said, "Yo, you got a good team man!" I remained impressed with the way the kids continued to play well against other kids, other teams, and other styles, achieving recognition.

It was hard to imagine we completed a baseball game close to 11:00 p.m. Who could have believed we'd still be playing baseball with Thanksgiving and Christmas coming up?

Glory over Gorillas

We headed back to the Bronx for our second game in the indoor tournament and faced the Gorillas. I was a little surprised to see our opponent practicing in the outside field (it was a spectacular morning weather wise, and many questioned why we didn't play outside). The Gorillas came from Manhattan (Coach John asked one of their coaches where they were from, and he replied "lower Manhattan" without specifying an area). The tournament organizer told John that last year's Gorillas were good and this year they "came bigger," so we were anticipating a showdown. The organizer also added that last week's game against GunHill was probably the least amount of talent we would see and the rest of the games would be competitive. This, more than anything, hyped Harry up.

Unfortunately the game was behind schedule, as there was another game taking place. The parents who were watching—about as large a crowd of spectators as we generally had—were loud, proud, and obnoxious, and for a second there, I had to make sure our parents were not there. I went outside to the practice field and saw a sea of red—parents, kids, and siblings with their red "What the Heck" sweatshirts (we are a fashionable bunch).

As the home team, the Gorillas take the indoor field, and their pitcher starts with two immediate strikeouts of Jack and Derek. Sosa is up. By this time, his family, including aunts, uncles, and cousins, has arrived. The talk throughout the day was of this being "his team," and I smile. He earns a walk. Wamcash smacks the ball, earning a double, and Jason walks.

We bat with the bases loaded. Harry would give signs at third base as to whether to "take a pitch" or not, and I recall a previous time a player was up with the bases loaded. A dad said within earshot, "Harry doesn't let him swing at the first pitch, and that was beautiful." After the kid struck out, the dad presumably blamed Harry. The pitches are nice, but the result is the same, and I'm not sure if there's anyone to blame.

In the bottom of the second, Jason pitches and gets a couple of strikeouts, followed by a nice catch by Marty at third base.

Jacob hits a nice shot at the top of the second. Stan moves him to third, and Edgar walks. Jack and Derek walk, and Sosa strikes out. Wamcash gets another hit, and errors by the Gorillas result in runs for us. The kids are yelling (not singing) their song—"We are Tayneck, mighty, mighty Tayneck!" The Gorilla coaching staff (sounds funny) calls time-out and tells the umpire the noise is annoying the pitcher. (It's annoying the moms of these kids, let alone the Gorillas.) I'm frantically calling Harry to remind him that, while the kids can sing, they can remain tasteful and not sound like a bunch of gorillas. Coach John sarcastically gets up every time the kid pitches, saying "shhhhhhhhhhhh" to the team. Although Jason strikes out, we end the inning having scored three, and Tayneck is up 3–0.

Jason strikes out two batters, and the defense holds its own. The Gorillas don't score in the bottom of the second.

Next, the Gorillas have their own 1–2–3 inning when Marty, Jacob, and Stan all get out.

In the bottom of the third, Marty makes a nice play to Mac at first, and I rightfully dub it an "M&M play" (as the candy coincidentally was being passed around). Again the Gorillas are scoreless.

It's the top of the fourth. Eddie hits. Mac hits, and the Gorilla's huge second baseman falls down and doesn't catch it. Then Jack walks. With the bases loaded, Derek walks, scoring one. Sosa hits and scores Mac. Wamcash scores, Jason walks, and Marty's out. Stan hits, and by the end of the inning, we are up 8–0.

Harry brings in Edgar to pitch at the bottom of the fourth. Derek is in centerfield, and Jack in second makes a beautiful stop and gets out of the inning. Again, the Gorillas are scoreless.

Top of the fifth—Mac earns a walk, as does Jack, and Derek strikes out. Sosa gets a hit, and we score two. Coach Sonny yells, "It's time to put some wood on the fire!" to rile the kids to hit. We're up 10–0.

But the Gorillas get one last chance to come up to bat. They face Edgar again, and he gets three quick outs. The game's over at 10–0.

Harry told the organizer he hoped tomorrow's game would start as scheduled at 6:00 p.m. It was a Sunday night, and we had to get the kids home and ready for bed and school the next day.

Harry also told me the team we'd be facing next was ready for us. He said that, if we won, we'd be sending a statement.

Developing Pitchers

FOR THE NEXT GAME OF the winter tournament we played the Scrappers and lost. While the loss seemed monumental to some parents, Harry seemed undisturbed. He believed the kids, specifically Derek, who led the team in strikeouts (ouch), were overmatched by the fast pitching of the almost always older kids. Derek summed it up when he conceded, "I was scared up there."

Jack walks, and after a quick strikeout by Derek, Wamcash singles. Stefon, Jason, and Sosa hit, and Marty is out but allows a run to score. Since the umpire never called time-out, Harry tells Sosa, "Go, go, go, go," and he scores. With a confused look on his face, the pitcher shows the umpire the ball, and the manager, who's yelling, wants to know what happened. The umpire explains that he never called time, so the ball was still in play and Sosa scored. While the umpire and manager are talking, Harry talks to Jacob.

The umpire yells, "Play ball!" and the game continues. Harry sends Wamcash home. Jacob hits but is called out—but not before we've scored five runs.

Marty takes the mound in the bottom of the second, and because of a throwing error by Derek, a runner arrives safely at first base. Derek makes up for the error when he starts a double play. The third batter hits it directly to Marty, and he's out at first. The score remains 5–0.

It's the top of the second, and Eddie hits. Edgar gets a hit, but the catcher ran interference, so the umpire calls Edgar safe at first and Eddie at second. Unfortunately, Jack, Derek, and Wamcash all strike out to end the inning.

Marty's still pitching, and while the batter hits it to right field, Edgar gets the ball into second base in time for the runner to stay on first. A hit to Wamcash gets the second out. And after a walk, the next batter hits the ball to Derek, who converts the out at first.

We bat at the top of the third, and Jason hits another shot to the outfield. Sosa hits, and Marty and Jacob strike out. Eddie hits the ball hard, but the right fielder catches it, and again, we leave runners on base.

At the bottom of the third, I panic when I see who's taking the mound. I wonder as I bite my nails why Derek is pitching, and I remember an earlier conversation about "developing other pitchers." I groan when he walks the first two batters. A hit to Wamcash, who holds the ball, results in Harry yelling, "What are you *doing!*" The opponent scores. Then Derek strikes one out and gets the ball hit to him for the out.

At the bottom of the third, we're up 6–I, and during the top of the fourth, the score remains the same.

Derek's still pitching in the bottom fourth, and I'm running out of nails. A hit to the outfield by a chubby kid actually materializes into an out, as Jack snaps the ball back to the first. Derek turns to Jack and gives him the thumbs-up (good sportsmanship). Derek walks then hits a batter, so with one out, the Gorillas have runners on first and second. I call Luis over so I can start biting his nails, as I have none left. The Gorillas score another run, and I stand from my chair. I'm taking notes and trying to videotape, and I tell a mom I'm nervous. She assures me it will be okay, and Derek gets a runner out.

In the top of the fifth, Jason hits another shot and gets to first but is out when Harry sends him to steal second. Sosa is out when he hits the top of the bubble. Marty is out. The score's now 6–2.

Harry brings in Sosa to pitch. The first batter hits and is out. The second hits to Derek at second but beats the throw and the Gorillas have a runner on first. Derek is flabbergasted and has Coach Nino and Harry telling him to calm down. The third batter hits to Jacob at first, and he's out.

At the top of the sixth, Jacob is out at first. Eddie and Edgar both walk. Jack strikes out. Derek walks, and with bases loaded, Wamcash strikes out.

Sosa goes in to pitch at the bottom of the sixth. The hit goes directly by him, but Derek is there to catch the ball and get the kid out at first. Harry remarks, "Thank your infield," and Sosa turns to Derek to thank him.

The kid batting up next apparently played at first base and then was a designated hitter. The umpire tells the manager, "You can't do that." I'm wondering why Harry is not arguing about the big kid coming up to bat. Harry is on one knee holding the bat, his trademark stance, and is not saying a word.

The kid hits a shot, which misses the home run mark by an inch, and the ball bounces in front of Stefon. Jack, who is in centerfield, gets the ball. And while the big boy thought he could get a double out of the hit, Jack throws it to Sosa, who's covering second, and the kid is out! The last kid up to bat hits to Jacob, and the final score is 6–2.

Coach gathers the kids to end the game with a "Neck problems, ballin'" chant, and a disapproving dad curls his lip.

We lost in the play-offs on December 9, 2006, 240 days after we started the incredible 2006 season on April 13, 2006. In those eight months we shared a lot of innings, games, and memories.

2007-10U

Recap

FOR THE 2007 SEASON, WE played 10U baseball. Harry decided to go with only three coaches in the dugout (him, John, and Alan). We welcomed a new player, Isaac, to the team and were supposed to play weekly. However, games were routinely cancelled, and unfortunately, we didn't play a Mother's Day game for the dedicated moms.

We headed back to Hackensack to participate in the Memorial Day Tournament. For the past two years, this team made it to the championship, and we entered again, hoping to make it to that elusive game. Harry felt we got screwed in the brackets; we had to play two games on Saturday, one starting at 8:00 a.m. and the other at noon against, you guessed it, Watson. Commonsense would dictate that the number one and number two teams two years in a row would be placed in separate brackets to determine if they have what it takes to meet again in the championship game.

On Saturday morning, we got to the field early and mercied the team, winning our first game. Under our big blue tent, we offered the kids oranges and grapes while we waited for Watson to finish their game before our scheduled noon game. All winter long, the kids had talked about waiting to face Watson, but I don't know what happened when they finally did—could it be fear?

Watson won the coin toss and was the home team. We batted first and were able to score a run.

In the bottom of the first, Harry brought in Sosa to pitch. However he looked sad when his dad left after the first game.

Sosa was on the mound, and wasn't smiling, though the moms begged him to. Harry would later reflect that had he known how hurt Sosa was by his dad's absence, he wouldn't have put him in to pitch.

During their half of that inning Watson scored five runs, thanks to two errors by our shortstop and an error by Derek. It was ugly. I stopped taking notes but can tell you that our kids didn't hit, were walking around with their shoulders slumped, and looked as if all of their dads had left. We lost, and Harry forecasted that we wouldn't make it to the championship game. Watson was now 2–0 and we were 1–1. Another powerhouse club team was in the tournament, and he figured they wouldn't lose.

Nonetheless, we continued playing. And our kids came right back with bats in their hands, hitting home runs. The final score of our next game was 22–2, but we (I) conceded our championship dream was over when Watson won their third game. They were headed to the championship game against the other team that was 3–0.

We were scheduled to play a consolation game for third place on Monday and would be facing the Roxbury Rangers. We started Mac to pitch and held them. Again, our bats came alive, and by the second inning, we were winning 10–1. At the bottom of the fifth, we brought in our closer, Wamcash. I guess it wasn't his day (or inning) because he walked in countless runners, and Roxbury came within one, ending the inning with a score of 10–9.

We were up to bat and started hitting again. This was also the first time Derek hit an in-the-park home run. I saw the ball hit far and started jumping up and down and yelling. When Harry stopped him at third and then waved him home, I jumped even higher. He ran so fast with those little legs and slid home so beautifully, missing the tag by a millisecond. The moms were high-fiving me, while his teammates ran out of the dugout to swarm him at home plate. For a baseball-loving mom like me who has seen her child struggle, it was great.

We won the game, 17–9, coming in third. And while we didn't make the championship game, the kids learned another lesson in character. A Watson pitcher who once struck Derek out, after which Derek came back again to get a hit—a situation that resulted in him and Derek frequently talking in between games (with Derek reminding him of the hit)—witnessed our hitting frenzy against Roxbury. I'm glad he got to see the real team and not the one that falls apart whenever they face Watson.

We would get another chance because we were scheduled to play Watson in our NJABC tournament in a couple of weeks. We would see what the boys learned and whether they had what it took to show the teams they were for real. At least one pitcher saw!

NJAABC Regional Tournament

DURING THE TOURNAMENT, WE PLAYED Mayfield and lost 4–10. We played against Watson and lost but beat Windham and Midland.

The NJAABC play-offs started, and Tayneck, who was hosting the regional, did not need to play because the hosting team got an automatic bid to play. Our parents showed extreme commitment and dedication as we worked together to get our fields ready. Coach John warned us that we had backup leagues and tournaments scheduled in the event we were eliminated.

Since we had no experience in hosting, much to everyone's surprise, the dedicated parents of the 10Us ran what everyone considered a successful tournament and were able to raise some funds for any necessary travel so we could continue to play baseball. While we didn't make it to Puerto Rico, we showed the township that we could run a tournament. It was refreshing to see the boys of the competitive Watson and Tayneck teams singing the national anthem at the championship game between Mayfield and Wolcott.

The 10U all-stars captured the New Jersey Amateur Baseball Conference North Jersey World Series crown by beating Fairfield 10–9 in an eight-inning thriller. The team went 4–0 in the tournament. Along the way, we beat Alexander, Watson, and Fairfield twice (once at their home and then at ours). The cute faces of the boys once again graced the local paper.

Cal Ripken Districts

THE RECREATION SEASON CAME TO an end, and it was time to embark on tournament play. Our local league became chartered with Babe Ruth/Cal Ripken, and we were playing in the districts. Coach John reminded us that ages ten and twelve were the big years in youth baseball, so it was time to make some noise and play some baseball. If we won the districts, we would advance to the states and then to the regionals in Spring City, Pennsylvania, with a world series in Indiana. There were no pitching limitations.

We played Clifton and won 25–0. Next up was Elmwood, and we won 5–0, with Wamcash pitching the whole game.

Game three was a little different. We played Babylon and lost 3–8. The game was more intense, and Harry was questioning the umpire's strike zone. I guess Harry's questioning was too much for the umpire, as he threw Harry out of the game. He later actually threatened to call the cops on Jacob's dad and Sonny (the nicest guy and our own motivational speaker!) because they would not stop commenting once Harry was out. The parents were yelling and questioning what was going on, and the normally in-your-face-coach John was eerily calm.

We played Elmwood in the semifinal and won 3–1. Since Harry got thrown out of a game, he was suspended from managing the championship game against Babylon, which we lost 2–4. Derek cried all the way home.

The team lost something more personal when our beloved Stefon moved to Georgia, despite pleas by the team to let him stay. Coach Harry gave him the team trophy during another team gathering at the Copley cabana.

We also entered the Durham Tournament and made it to the championship game against Oxford, which prompted a couple of dedicated parents to adjourn their vacation (twice). Our dedicated parents cheered when the kids were told by the umpire to stop.

We traveled to Yaphank, New York, for Baseball Heaven and took over the pool at the Islandia Marriott. This weekend tournament produced lots of laughter and a new cheer—"contra-ataque." Hearing the Spanish cheers directed to Mac, who was on the mound probably wondering what the heck those crazy parents were saying, was quite hysterical.

In district 4 tournament regular games, we almost beat Bennington, blanked Elmwood, and lost to Harrington. Thankfully, we won our first play-off game against Harrington 5–2 without getting one solo hit.

During fall baseball as an IIU team, Harry was elected president of the baseball board. I had established softball for our league and ventured into managing on my own with Coach Alan assisting me. I was humbled when awarded the prestigious Volunteer of the Year award.

Almost six months exactly to the date of our first game, we played a semifinal game.

We started with a 3–0 lead, but the opponent tied the game. Their oversized player hit a three-run home run and took the lead.

The boys didn't give up. It was a cold night, and scorekeeping Coach Dennis had a box of hot chocolate in the dugout. The kids were able to hit their big pitcher, but unfortunately, we were unable to capitalize with bases loaded in the bottom of the sixth down 3–6, and the game ended. The Big Red Machine concluded its season. A lot of the boys walked away with tears in their eyes for the way the full season ended.

We were a happy team, and the parents appreciated the efforts of the coaches to make the kids smile, even after a loss. The kids still went home feeling like they accomplished something and still wanted to play baseball again. It was nice to read parent e-mails commenting on how our team was special, how the boys were learning more than baseball, and how our memories were priceless.

SUMMER AND FALL
2008-11U

Burnout and "Beach" Blast

LUIS STARTED PLAYING 8U TRAVEL baseball, and my scorekeeping skills were authenticated when Harry asked me to join him in the dugout as the scorekeeping coach. For the love of the game (and to give Luis the same baseball attention that he'd given Derek), Harry managed two travel teams. He endured twice the amount of questioning from parents who wanted to know why their child had sat, was batting last, or had not been made "permanent shortstop" or to remind him that their boy preferred the infield over the outfield. For the most part, he was dealing sanely with the frenzy. But things were changing, and we lost one of our original players, Wamcash, to a club baseball team.

In July 2008, Harry had to deal with two unfortunate instances when moms on each team made public scenes. When one child was substituted and sat in the dugout, the dad stormed off. That was when the mom publicly expressed her displeasure. The other, believing her child had been treated unfairly, went to the local newspaper. When a reporter sought Harry for a comment on the situation, he refused to provide one, saying only, "This is youth baseball. Why would I give a comment to the newspapers?" The newspaper then sought a comment from one of the board members, and as expected, the board wasn't happy.

The board mandated that all travel teams conduct mandatory parent meetings before a season started to remind all about the Parents Code of Conduct, which encourages parents to be role models and set positive examples. My Pollyanna view was disintegrating, and these interactions were brewing in me a negative sentiment. Harry withdrew, feeling burned out and down, and for several days, the team seemed in limbo. I was losing the passion and excitement that had once filled me, so I was thankful for a baseball experience with the team, who displayed true valor and the ability to bounce back. It was about the kids, damn it!

Why the tournament was called the Jersey Shore Beach Blast was unclear, as we didn't see a beach near the field. The only beach we saw was on Thursday night when my family drove down to Point Pleasant to walk by the boardwalk. We reserved rooms at a Courtyard Marriot about twenty minutes away. Harry, the kids, and I arrived a night earlier.

On the Fourth of July, Coach Alan advised us via text that "the Neck" had arrived and the team was down at the field waiting to play.

We won the first game against the Two River Dawgs by more than ten runs, including a home run by Jason. The game was over a lot sooner than we expected, so a lot of the parents decided to leave to check into the hotel, and the others got some lunch and/or went shopping.

We got back to the field by 5:30 and awaited the start of the second game.

We were to face Mount Lorraine. As I walked past their dugout, I overheard their coach telling the team that, since their pitcher "looked strong," they would be able to "no hit" the Tayneck team and head out quickly. I made it a point to tell our coaches this to pump them up some more (not that they needed it, as Coach John replied, "The *Two* River Dawgs got *one* ass whooping").

Mac was the starting pitcher. I don't know what happened to Mac, or if anything happened to him, but they hit the ball. It was like they found whatever gap they could and just shot the ball over there. Although we had our own offensive display with two home runs by Sosa and Stan, and they didn't get to "no hit" us, we lost 4–14. Our two games were done and we would play two on Saturday.

We were scheduled to play the Shore Hurricanes at 10:45, but earlier rain pushed the game back.

Marty pitched but did not find the strike zone and walked a lot of batters. The Hurricanes took the lead, but thankfully, again with home runs by Sosa and hits by our team, we won 16–8.

We grabbed some lunch and headed back to play the Colts Neck Stampede later in the afternoon. Derek pitched four innings and allowed no runs. This was good for Derek, who was struggling with hitting and defense. Harry had all these theories about why Derek was "regressing" in his game, but I thought he was just ten years old. I was happy about his great pitching performance and his bunt to score a run because I saw his confidence coming back. We won 10–0.

The championship game was scheduled for 9:00 a.m. We were the second seed, since our record was 3–1, and Mount Lorraine was the top seed, with a 4–0 record. If Mount Lorraine won Sunday morning, they would be the champions. If we won, we'd have to play a second game at 11:30. I got Derek and Luis to bed, knowing we had to get up early. Harry told me he was glad the boys would walk away with a trophy, either second or first place. Four games of baseball played well and the chance to win a championship was fantastic.

On Sunday morning, the fog was unbelievable, and I wondered how the boys were going to see the baseball, let alone catch it. But the game couldn't be changed. Two umpires would be officiating, and I was worried, as the younger field umpire let it be known that he would not take any talk and would throw Harry (or John) out of the game.

I don't think Mount Lorraine expected what happened. I believe they expected to win quickly. Sosa was the starting pitcher and completely took control. The pitching was perfect, our defense was tight, and the hits were timely. They scored one first, and we were able to tie up the game in the fourth inning. You could see the look of panic on their faces, as they could see the game slipping away.

After Sosa, Harry brought in Edgar to pitch, and he held them.

At the top of the fifth, Stan hit a home run, and we were up 2–1. Edgar held them down, and we won the game. Mount Lorraine was forced to play a second game at 11:30 a.m.

There was no time to eat, so we were running into the cars for snacks and drinks. I overheard a mom saying on her cell phone that they couldn't make a commitment; they hadn't expected to play two games. (Hah!)

Harry brought in Jason to pitch. They scored one, and we held them. In between innings, I saw Derek, who was playing left field instead of second base, looking down. (Harry thought Derek was becoming afraid of the balls at second base—some of these players were double his size and hit hard.) I asked him what was wrong. He said, "I'm not getting any action in left field."

"Be careful what you wish for," I told him.

After a couple of great running plays, we were able to tie it up 1–1 in the fourth inning. Jason pitched four innings. At the end of the fourth inning, they scored again, and they were up 1–2. Jason's mom asked me whether Harry would put her son into pitch the fifth. "It's the championship, baby," I told her. "All bets are off." I also reminded Jason, "You're pitching in a championship game—can't ask for anything better."

I almost fell out of my seat when I saw Derek take the mound and thought Harry had lost his mind. Derek was ten; we had a twelve-year-old and four eleven-year-olds on the team, so why would he bring in Derek? He would later explain to me, "Derek throws strikes," which is what was needed. I could feel and taste the vomit in my mouth, as I was petrified for my little Derek. I was so afraid he wasn't going to do well, and I worried what that would do for him (and for the car ride back home). That fear slowly dissipated as I saw the confidence he had. He was throwing strikes, striking kids out, and smiling on the mound. My eyes welled up with tears; my baby was going to be okay. I figured Harry was going to let him pitch one inning and then bring in Mac to close.

After successfully ending the inning, we came up to bat. Sosa hit a beautiful home run to tie the game. I got up from my beach chair to cheer, dizzy from the quick jump and probably because my emotions, ranging from panic, fear, and shock to pride and happiness, were all rolled together.

We were tied 2–2 going into the bottom of the sixth inning. I saw Derek back up on the mound and sat back down. I couldn't take the pressure, but I saw my little boy, my little champ, smile as he got on the mound. Two outs. One more to go. And then if we went into extra innings, Harry would get somebody else to pitch (please). I couldn't take the pressure, so I didn't talk. I bent my head down to pray, not so much that the team would win but that my boy would be okay. An error by the shortstop resulted in a runner on first base. Derek looked a bit disturbed, but he was told by his coaches to "throw strikes." He threw a strike to the next batter, who hit the ball to the right field. The fielder missed it. The runner on first made it home. Mount Lorraine won.

The team lined up to shake hands, and Derek cried. My heart bled, but I couldn't help but cheer and clap with the rest of the parents (on both sides), who had just witnessed two outstanding baseball games—no double digit scores but two classic one-run games.

The boys got second place trophies, and Derek, red-eyed, was sitting alone. I sat next to him and told him I was proud. I reminded him that he was one of the youngest on the team but had been on that mound trying to finish the championship game. More than that, he hadn't allowed his hitting slump to get him down. He'd contributed to the team the way he could.

Harry gave the championship trophy to Sosa for his contribution with the home runs (four total) and his pitching. Sosa got teary-eyed.

As I tucked Derek into bed, he asked, "I pitched good, right, Mom?" While I acknowledged that he had, more than anything, I reminded him that he hadn't given up.

The summer was challenging, and it seemed the team family was changing. This weekend was essential for me to feel the excitement of the team, witness the never-quit attitude, win more games, and get another trophy. More importantly, it helped me realize what was vital in life—not necessarily baseball but what it was teaching me. Maybe the lesson was that we should continue to show up and fight back, despite the negative. I had two kids, a good husband, a great family, and a nice life. Anything else was icing on the cake.

Yes, We Can!

WE TRAVELED DOWN TO YAPHANK to participate in the Labor Day Weekend Baseball Heaven tournament. For away tournaments, I began preparing a "packet" of information, with directions, schedules, and a list of items to bring. The night before we left, history was made, when forty-five years after Martin Luther King's famous "I Have a Dream" speech, Barack Obama accepted the Democratic nomination for president, which stirred me deeply. I watched his speech, spent hours watching the analysis, and realized at 1:15 a.m. that I hadn't sent the packet. I prepared it, and with all the emotions stirring inside me, used as my sound bite, "Yes, we can," in deference to history just made.

With the "Yes, we can" packet of information in hand, we set out. The facility had improved since we were last there. More fields had been established, along with areas to sell food. Harry knew there was a game scheduled for Friday night, so we went to watch. Although the parents arrived that night, given my lack of sleep and what would be an early appearance at the field (7:15 a.m.), I wasn't in the mood to socialize. Instead, I went to bed early.

The tournament began with ten teams, and our first game was against the Island Bulldogs. We beat the team 16-1 and, given the amount of runs, the mercy rule came into effect and we were done in three innings with strong pitching and a solid offensive attack. I coordinated several hours of play for the families at the local Dave & Buster's, where we ate and let the kids play video games. The boys were scheduled to play two games on Sunday, again starting at 8:00 a.m. and then 10:00 a.m., so we suggested (pretty strenuously) that the boys get their required rest.

Again we were at the field at 7:15 a.m. We played Rosedale and tied 8-8. Immediately following that game, we played the Belleville All Stars and lost 0–9.

I had scheduled Derek's pizza birthday party following the games, but the mood didn't appear celebratory and parents seemed angry.

We entered the fourth regularly scheduled game with one win, one loss, and one tie. As the second seed in a pool, we were scheduled to play the undefeated champion in a semifinal game.

The Hurricanes jumped to a 0–5 lead, and after an inning and a half, it looked like we were done. The team stormed back with five runs in the bottom of the second. This was a game that oozed determination. Center fielder Marty stopped a rally with a sliding catch of a sinking liner for the third out of the inning. Derek provided four 1/3 innings of shutout relief to get the win.

We advanced to the championship game with a 6–5 victory, but not before Harry was thrown out of the game by the umpire. Watching one of the parents tell Harry what was going on while he sat in the car was comical, and Harry seemed to manage the game via cell phone. Superstition kicked in, and we were all supposed to stay in the same place!

For the championship game, we jumped to a 2–0 lead in the top of the first and never looked back. We won the championship game 5–2 and headed home close to 10:00 p.m. As one parent recalled, the kids were determined to win without Harry, and it was like his spirit was ingrained in them. The lateness of the hour didn't matter. We had won the tournament dramatically!

A couple of weeks later, the coaches surprised the boys with T-shirts that read, "Baseball Heaven Labor Day Tournament Champions 2008." (Derek's wardrobe of tournament T-shirts listing our involvement was starting to overflow.) The shirt had the scores of the game and listed the players' names and uniform numbers. Derek wore it proudly.

Cal Ripken Tournament

We headed to Aberdeen, Maryland, for the Cal Ripken Tournament. Our first game was scheduled for 9:00 a.m., which required an early wake-up call and early breakfast. We were the visiting team, and Lehigh obnoxiously changed our "What time is it" cheer to "What team are we."

Derek starts with a walk to first base, and Jason moves him to third (after he stole second). After Marty strikes out, Sosa hits a shot to outfield, but it is caught.

Mac pitches in the top of the first inning, and the first kid is out. But then a shot by the second batter gets him to second, and they score two in the first inning.

We bat in the top of the second, but Mac, Stan, and Jack all get out. We hold them in the bottom of the second.

It's the top third, and Isaac and Jacob get out. But Edgar and Eddie each hit to left field. Derek walks. With the bases loaded, Jason gets a hit that scores two. Marty walks, and the bases are loaded again. This time, Sosa's up to bat. He hits to left field, and the fielder ends up hitting Jason for the third out. The game is tied 2–2, and Lehigh doesn't score during the bottom of the third.

We're up to bat. Mac hits to center field and tries to steal second but is out. Stan walks but is caught stealing second, and there are two outs. Jack walks, and Isaac singles after the pitcher falls down trying to catch the steal. Jacob hits to right field, scoring Jack and Isaac. Edgar gets out.

In the bottom of the fourth, they score three after a single and errors by Sosa and Marty. They lead 4–5. We ask them to please hit to complement the errors! Coach Alan talks to them. Jacob gets a ten for the split he makes while catching the ball.

We don't score during the top of the fifth; after Eddie strikes out, Derek grounds to short, and Marty grounds to short. In the bottom of the fifth, we get three quick outs, and they don't score.

We score two in the top sixth, with Sosa getting hit by a pitch, Mac getting a single, and Stan striking out. Jack moves a runner over with a bunt but starts crying because he didn't get on base, and Harry reminds him this was a much needed sacrifice play. Isaac gets a hit.

We are winning 6–5 when Lehigh comes up to bat the bottom of the sixth and don't score. We come up to bat at the top of the seventh, and we don't score.

When the bottom of the seventh rolls around, Mac's still pitching. But Harry, who never wants to have a kid pitch excessively, asks him to finish the bottom of the order. The first kid hits a shot to left field, which hits Isaac.

We make a pitching change, and Sosa walks the first batter, so he has first and second. The next batter gets a single that Jacob bobbles. He strikes out the next batter, and it's one out. A grounder to first base gets the second out. The kid at first tries to steal, and Jason throws the ball to Mac during the run down. Mac tags the kid, but when the umpire runs over, he hears the opposing coach yell, "Safe!" and coincidentally yells, "Safe!" thereafter.

Dads start yelling, "*Walk off the field! That's ridiculous!*"

Harry is trying to get everybody to calm down. The opposing parents are yelling, "*Here we go . . .,*" making fun of our cheer. Harry tries to speak to the umpire, but the call remains.

The umpire warns us we've reached the two-hour limit. The last kid hits a grounder to first, and the game ends in a tie. In Maryland, *no, we didn't.*

2009 SEASON-12U

The Final Year (On and Off the Field):
Live the Dream

THE YEAR IN YOUTH BASEBALL considered most significant is the age of twelve. This is the last time players play on the "small" baseball field, as they progress to the "big field," which measures sixty-by-ninety, at the age of thirteen. During 2009, we played in leagues, districts, and tournaments and again were successful and welcomed two additions to the team. A coach Harry had played against who liked our team presented him with an opportunity for a great experience for the kids. Before they left the small field, they could play in the legendary home of baseball, Cooperstown, New York.

Harry was offered a bid to play in the Cooperstown Dreams Park Tournament. This tournament was like no other. I overheard a dad call it the "baseball bar mitzvah." It was an entire week of baseball (we had done weekend tournaments) and would require the kids and coaches to stay in the barracks and the parents to rent houses or apartments together for a week. The costs were also different than what we had seen, as the tournament would cost several hundred dollars per player. We agreed to prepare a souvenir journal to help defray expenses. The price included the cost of staying for a week at the barracks, uniforms, the food, and a priceless ultimate baseball experience. The kids would also be inducted into the Youth Baseball Hall of Fame.

Harry assembled a parent meeting to discuss as a team whether we should go. The parents collectively decided to go, and since Harry had been questioned about playing time he wanted their agreement on a planned addition. He was concerned that, with a weeklong tournament, we'd need extra pitchers and players, and an extra player would help. Harry wanted one of our original players, Stefon, who had moved to Georgia, to participate in this experience with us. Who better than Steady Stefon?

The group agreed to allow Stefon to come, with some requisite e-mails reminding Harry that some would be expected to play more than he. The disclaimers on playing time aside, parents appeared excited, probably more than the kids. Groups of parents had rented accommodations and would stay together. Harry reminded parents who believed we could win it all that it wasn't so much about winning but about competing. A win could occur. I shared a house with the wives of the coaches, who were in the barracks.

There were teams from Canada (and both the Canadian national anthem and our national anthem were played), along with California, Georgia, Florida, and New York, among others. The founder of the Dreams Park talked about what the building of this park, established in 1996, meant to him and his family. It featured manicured baseball fields, barracks for the teams to sleep in, dining halls for the kids to eat in, and pin trading areas. The park's mantra was "Dreaming the Dream," and that mantra was mentioned on many occasions, including a vast sign "Live the Dream" painted on one of the buildings.

The opening ceremony was spectacular. I was standing in the bleachers with many of our parents. One of our moms (who on several occasions criticized Harry about his coaching skills and the playing time her son received) was next to me and said emotionally, "I just can't believe this," tears in her eyes.

As a parent (and baseball lover), when you sit in a baseball field (or football field, soccer field, or any other field where your child plays), having witnessed wins, losses, errors that demoralize a team, team huddles, and coaches screaming, you hope all those moments lead to something your child remembers forever. Being in Cooperstown, the home of baseball, watching hundreds of people in the stands cheering for 105 teams from all over the country, and knowing that *your* child plays a part, would bring emotions to even the coolest of hearts.

As if the baseball gods had planned it, we were amused to see our old friends from Watson participating at the same time we were, but this time as a club team. I wondered if they'd ever imagined, during the close games we'd played, that we would end up meeting up in the home of baseball. I doubt it, but then again, sillier dreams have happened.

We looked at the sky and saw three air gliders jump off a plane, gliding down onto the field dressed in baseball uniforms. Then the parade of champions began. One hundred and five teams in alphabetical order walked down from the barracks dressed in red, white, and blue. I brought an eleven-by-fourteen picture I had of Derek; I wanted him to see I was proud. I was trying to videotape, console the mom who by now was completely blubbering, and ensure I didn't fall from the bleachers, as the jumping up and down and cheering was out of control. I put the camera down, picked up the picture, and made sure Harry saw what I was doing. He directed Derek to look at me. When Derek saw me holding his photo, his smile was remarkable. He was one of several holding the league banner, and I will never forget the smile on his face.

The skills competition was next, and Derek was selected for the "Golden Arm" competition, where the boys had three chances to throw a ball from centerfield into a red hole by home plate. Players were awarded points for the amounts of times they hit the box. Derek was number 85 of 105 selected, and we sat and watched. Many of the other boys were bigger than Derek, and some weren't able to get it anywhere near the target. I was videotaping, so I couldn't see where Derek was throwing them, but I heard the sound of a ball hitting a wood board at least once and was very happy to hear a player standing to my left say, "Man, that kid has an arm," when Derek threw it from centerfield past the wooden board. Although he hit it one time, he was eliminated.

After hanging with the parents and siblings trading pins, the moms left for the dark drive back to the rental. I searched for any location in the house where Internet service was available, but when I saw cows and bulls up the street and pig clocks *all over* the house, I presumed that Internet service and this décor probably did not mix. So I tried to handwrite some notes.

The boys played six games and were seeded for the play-offs. We won two games out of six and ranked 38 out of 105. We beat a team from Massachusetts, and Harry was able to get all the kids some playing time, although it wasn't uncommon for kids to come out of the dugout at the end of the game looking sad. Maybe they didn't play as much as they wanted to. Some kids hit home runs, and others came close. By the time the play-offs were over, we were ranked 52 out of 105. For a town team competing against club teams from all over the country, it was an amazing experience—one Harry was happy to have shared with the team.

The Beginning of the End

It was common for parents to suggest to Harry what he should do with a player, and Harry, to his credit, would listen. If a dad told Harry, "Junior is better off playing the infield or is a great pitcher," Harry would eventually move Junior to that position. If, however, Junior didn't do well or made errors, just as Junior's dad had felt free to talk to Harry about the player, Harry in turn would do the same; and in his honest, irreverent manner he would remind the parent of the glowing recommendation he'd given.

The e-mails, texts, and comments Harry received before and after a game about positions, batting lineup, and pitching availability were increasing. It seemed that, no matter what he was doing, despite the fact that the team was winning, Harry was never winning with some parents. They were being honest with him. He couldn't be honest with them.

Following our return from Cooperstown, with the baseball bar mitzvah over, for fall baseball, the kids would be introduced to the bigger baseball field. They had outgrown (and aged out of) the forty-six-by-sixty (or fifty-by-seventy) field and now had to try to pitch from sixty feet, run ninety-foot bases, and make throws in a wider playing field. Derek, a league twelve-year-old, would make the switch despite his age. Harry was asked at a team meeting if, given Derek's age, he was still going to move the *team* up to the bigger field, and he said yes. I would realize later why the question was asked.

We played in a tournament with games held during the week. Parental attendance was down, given the school/work week and the colder weather. I saw the parents whisper to each other but didn't give it much thought. Despite our new field of play, the kids were adapting and won a couple of games, but along with decreasing parental attendance, players stopped attending, and many times, with not enough to field a team, we forfeited.

Sports at the Beach—The "Team" Washed Away

WE TRAVELED TO THE SPORTS at the Beach Tournament in Delaware. We won the two pool play games and got a bye for the play-offs. Harry would tell the team to meet him at the batting cages before the game, but kids or parents wouldn't show up, instead meeting another dad on another cage to practice. Being the naive person I was, I didn't realize what was happening. The whispers and mingling continued, but given my gnawing knot of uneasiness, I didn't mind that I was not included.

For play-off game number one, Harry picked Eddie to pitch. Harry advised me afterward that he wanted to save others for further play-off games, and after a talk with and stats provided by Eddie's dad, he figured Eddie was an appropriate choice.

After a quick first out, Eddie walked the next two, and with wild pitches, our opponents were in scoring position. Four hits later and the entire lineup batting, by the bottom of the first, we were down 0–5. We scored two, but when the opponent batted again, they scored some more. We ultimately lost 6–13. Unlike other games, where parents assembled to talk, this time, parents left unsettled and unhappy.

On November 7, 2009, we played a game in the fall league. Little did I know, this would be the last game for this team. No speeches, no cupcakes, no parents gathering to talk—it would just end. I innocently stumbled across photos in that cauldron of openness—Facebook— of several players wearing different uniforms and, obviously, playing the game as another team. I was stunned. I could not believe they could play elsewhere but probably more selfishly felt shut out. I thought Harry knew but had failed to tell me.

When Harry came home, I said, "Did you know your team is playing somewhere else?"

He just stared at me, and his reaction was a mixture of shock, anger, hurt, disdain, and bewilderment. He walked away and mumbled, "This is why I didn't want any friends."

We attempted to get answers as to what happened, but the story was confusing and haphazard. Several parents justified their decision to abandon Harry (and John along with him) by suggesting that since the team would have to move to a bigger field, they believed Harry wouldn't move along with it, given that Derek (and Jack) were twelve. But a parent had asked his plans on the matter at a parent meeting, and he'd affirmed that the team would move up and stay together. No matter the rationale, the bottom line was this—the mighty town team; the band of brothers; the family; the warriors who had fought through so many hurdles, played baseball, and compiled trophies was no longer together. As quick as you could say, "Play ball," the parents said to Harry (and John), "You're out!"

Derek sadly asked, "Why can't I play on this team?"

But I didn't have an answer.

Conclusion

WAS THE BREAKUP HARRY'S FAULT? I honestly don't think so, although I spent a lot of time subconsciously blaming him for an honest demeanor and attitude that could have offended. However, this demeanor and attitude produced success. Countless trophies later (and team trophies to almost every player) was the culmination of his hard work and determination to get the kids to play among the best. Parents have the right to decide what is best for their children. But after years of proclaiming ourselves a family and unique as we stayed together despite the epidemic of other teams surfacing, the concealed dissolution of the team seemed unjust. Harry and John deserved better. Parents opted to have their kids play elsewhere. While that was disappointing, their decision to cover the move up and isolate us added insult to injury. To find out the way we did and hear conflicting stories about how "everybody knew" and "Harry broke up the team" was wrong. Through the years, parents commented on the joy of having our kids learn lessons on honesty, integrity, and true spirit, and I sadly wondered if some parents missed the class.

A coach once said, "They warned me not to get into this business." And his comment is amusing because he was talking youth baseball. Travel baseball is *huge*! I've learned that adults can obsess about their kid's playing time and will do what is necessary to hand their child that revered position or more playing time. But life isn't that easy. I have seen parents pull out all the stops to ensure that their child has a head start to succeed, whether in the youth arena, as the starting shortstop at the high school, as a recipient of a college scholarship, or maybe even in the major leagues. Yes, the kids should dream the dream, as so eloquently stated in the Dreams Park. But somewhere down the road, that dream can, for some, turn into a nightmare.

Given his tough exterior, Harry never admitted how much the loss hurt. I know it took a lot out of him, and I was constantly reminded that he only wanted an opportunity to coach kids and not make friends. With the other team, the stressful e-mails were continuing. As sad as it was, he was cursed out, talked about, and maligned. But he forged ahead in his quest to teach players to compete. He continued to coach Luis, but remained cautious about parents and their agendas and reacted differently. In the ultimate scheme of things, with what he'd gone through and survived, losing a team was not his end.

Derek struggled. His final memories of the team were sad ones and it pained me when he refused to sleep in his bedroom, which contained pictures, T-shirts, trophies, and mementos gained through the years. During a recreation game the following year, he struck out while being pitched to by a former teammate and was laughed at from the bleachers. I was devastated.

Harry, who was coaching first base, walked over to the kids and the parents and said, "This is what you're teaching them?" They were told to stop.

Derek cried that night and I held him until he fell asleep. He learned an unfortunate but early life lesson that life isn't fair and kids will be kids. Derek, Jack, Harry, and John would start again and, given the loss of town players, they would venture into club baseball.

I have no regrets. The team was special, and it did feel unique. Everything I did—from sending parent e-mails and tournament packets to arranging hotels and organizing events outside tournaments—I did selflessly and for people I liked. This was family, and I would do anything for family. I am grateful for the vast memories we compiled, which innocently started by watching my son play my favorite game. As a team, we celebrated each other's birthdays; we went away, went rafting, watched Super Bowls, and brought in the New Year together; we celebrated grandparents' birthdays, visited kids in the hospital, and supported siblings who started playing; and, of course, we watched the boys play baseball. I lost contact, but as Harry reminds me, life goes on.

A mom reached out and told me she valued my friendship no matter where our kids played, which touched me. As much as it pained me, I, along with two other moms, finished the souvenir journal the team started for the Cooperstown trip. The journal that had taken so long to finalize was complete for delivery and symbolized, for me, the finality of the team. I personally hand delivered copies to the parents' mailboxes and felt my heart twist just a little bit. I was cheerless but quietly hoped I would receive answers as a result of delivering the journals. The silence was deafening, so I questioned how ridiculous it was for me to feel miserable when I no longer gathered with this group. But in truth, I mourned the loss of a big and significant part of my life. I loved the life I lived near that town baseball diamond. I loved the way the group assembled as the underdog but battled back successfully. It was an affirmation of my life's journey. Although in my beginning the toilet paper presents from my fabricated friends sufficed, the memories in my head made with these real people remains a priceless gem.

I still love town baseball and commend a group of kids staying together to achieve a goal. This "B" team stayed together, practiced, trained, played, and competed. The amount of games won through the years surpassed the losses, and many losses (sometimes even those against club teams) were close ones. The kids competed with *any* team—a goal Harry always had in mind, and he hopes he taught them in their continued baseball careers that they can face any opponent.

Only time will tell if I can trust again embark on a "club" baseball mom role with Derek and town team coach with Luis and am thankful I have softball managerial duties and girls to coach to occupy my time. I remain optimistic and hope I'll allow myself to trust again and report wide-eyed with eternal optimism that America's pastime, which has consumed my life, brings me joy.

I miss our team and the group and will savor the experiences, the games, the cheers, the victories, the celebrations, and the closeness the boys and families shared. For five fun-filled years, it felt as if I had many sons and my boys had that band of brothers. I'm comforted that my son made fabulous memories he can pass on and that, with hard work and dedication, can face any challenge or any opponent. When I think back to that original championship victory on that beautiful Sunday morning and the elation we all felt, I still smile. That season epitomized the lesson that, if you continue to show up despite being knocked down, it's possible that good things can happen. It also taught me that no matter what I did (cupcake baker and pizza-party organizer), sometimes it's the quiet spectators and fans who show up to support who get the game ball. It is possible to break the personal curse of the Bambinos. As our beloved Coach Sonny used to say, "Nobody beats you when you work hard." For a while, this team was the pride of the town. Life changes and people change, but for me, "What time is it?" carries a special meaning. Thankfully, the game of baseball doesn't change. What the heck?!